Financial Decision-Making

Financial Decision-Making

A Practical Guide for Resource Allocation
in Financial Institutions

BRIAN PIZZALA

Copyright © 1990 Brian Pizzala

All rights reserved. No part of this publication may be reproduced, stored in a retrieval system, or transmitted in any form or by any means, electronic, mechanical, photocopying, recording, or otherwise without the prior permission of the publishers.

First published in 1990
by the Mercury Books Division of
W.H. Allen & Co. Plc
Sekforde House, 175/9 St John Street, London EC1V 4LL

Set in Palatino by Phoenix Photosetting, Chatham
Printed and bound in Great Britain by
Mackays of Chatham PLC, Chatham, Kent

This book is sold subject to the condition that it shall not, by way of trade or otherwise, be lent, re-sold, hired out or otherwise circulated without the publisher's prior consent in any form of binding or cover other than that in which it is published and without a similar condition including this condition being imposed upon the subsequent purchaser.

British Library Cataloguing in Publication Data

Pizzala, Brian,
    Financial decision making: a practical
    guide for resource allocation in financial
    institutions.
    1. Great Britain. Investment by financial
    institutions.
    Portfolio analysis
    I. Title
    332.6'7154'0941

    ISBN 1–85251–003–X

CONTENTS

1 INTRODUCTION AND ACKNOWLEDGEMENTS
Introduction   1
Acknowledgements   2

PART ONE

2 BASICS OF DISCOUNTED CASHFLOW ANALYSIS
Measuring Profitability   5
Accounting Data   5
The Time Dimension   6
Present Value   7
Net Present Value   10
An Example   10
A Hidden Assumption   11
The True Rate of Return   12
Economic Depreciation   12

3 SHAREHOLDER VALUE
Rationale   15
Earnings and Dividends Compared   16
Retained Profits v Dividends   18
Average and Marginal Earnings Compared   19
Real and Nominal Returns   21
Is the Price/Earnings Ratio Meaningful?   22

4 COST OF EQUITY AND THE CAPITAL ASSET PRICING MODEL

Measuring Returns on Equity	25
Introduction	25
The Arithmetic Average	26
The Geometric Mean or Income Reinvested Method	27
UK Cost of Equity: an Alternative Approach	28
The Capital Asset Pricing Model	30
Theoretical Framework	30
The Capital Asset Pricing Model in Practice	33
Critique of the Capital Asset Pricing Model	35
Conclusions	37

5 TRADITIONAL CASHFLOW ANALYSIS

Why Cashflows?	38
Cashflow and Shareholder Value	40
Profits, Balance Sheets and Cashflows	41
Bygones are Bygones	45
Weighted Cost of Capital	46
Equity Flows	46
Weighted Cost of Capital	47
The Capital Asset Pricing Model Again	48
Repayment Assumptions	51

PART TWO

6 BANK REGULATION AND CAPITAL ADEQUACY

Introduction	55
Risk-weighted Assets	55
Conventional Contingents	56
Interest Rate and Foreign Exchange Contingents	56
An Example	57
Capital Adequacy	59
Equity: First Tier Capital	59
Second Tier Capital	59
Deductions from Capital	61

Contents

	The Minimum Capital Ratio	61
	Annex 1 Risk Weight Categories: On Balance Sheet	62
	Annex 2 Credit Conversion Factors: Conventional Contingents	65

7 THE BASIC BANKING MODEL

Equity Flows or Cashflows?	67
Back to Accounting Profits	68
A Basic Equity Flow Model	69
Accounting Profits and Cashflows Revisited	70
Opportunity Costs	72
Equity Injections	75
Second Tier Capital	76
Opportunity Costs with Second Tier Capital	77
Treatment of Second Tier Capital	78
Free Funding	80
Risk-weighted Assets	81
An Example	81
Terminal Values: A Conundrum	84
Introduction	84
Dividends in Perpetuity	84
Sale of Business	84
Recommended Approach	85

8 EXTENSIONS OF THE BANKING MODEL

Introduction	86
Goodwill	86
Minorities	87
Non-consolidated Investments	88
A Case Study: an Acquisition	88
Closure	91
Sale	92

9 INTERNATIONAL DIMENSIONS

Additional Considerations	94
Interest Rates	94
Foreign Exchange Movements	95

FINANCIAL DECISION-MAKING

Holding Gains	95
FX Gains and Holding Gains: an Example	95
Consistency of Assumptions	98
Inflation	98
Interest Rates	98
Implications for Project Appraisal	99
Local Accounting v Domestic Accounting	100
An Example	100
The Alone Balance Sheet	102

10 DEBT SWAPS

Debt Bond Swaps	105
Provisions Are Bygones	105
New Monies	107
Additional Provisions	108
Expected Values	108
The Model: Existing Debt	108
Bond Valuation	111
Comparative Economics	112
Debt Equity Swaps	114
An Alternative Approach Applied to Debt Property Swaps	116
General Considerations	116
The Swap	117
Valuing Debt: a Probability Interpretation	117
Valuing Property	118
Taxation	119
Debt-forgiveness	119

11 THE INTEGRATED MODEL

Basic Structure	121
Environmental Assumptions	122
The Balance Sheet and Contingents	124
Net Interest Income	124
Profit and Loss Account	127
Equity	129

Contents

12 EVALUATING FIXED ASSET EXPENDITURE

Back to Basics	130
Plant and Equipment: Basic Approach	130
The Supporting Balance Sheet	131
Investment in Property	134
Property Revaluations	135
Property Revaluations: Insufficient Secondary Capital	137
Sale of Premises	138
Two Examples	139
Annex Revaluations Contribute to First Tier Capital	144

13 PRICING

Rationale	146
The Supporting Balance Sheet Revisited	146
Derivation of the Basic Model	149
Extension of the Model	154
Fee Income	157
Average and Marginal Cost Pricing	159
External Pricing	159
Internal Marginal Cost Pricing	160
The Cost of Funds	162
Local and Domestic Returns	162
Relationship Profitability	164
Relative Risk	165
Bridging the Gap	167

14 THE COST OF EQUITY REVISITED

Introduction	171
Bank Betas	171
Calculating the Cost of Equity	172
Implications for Project Appraisal	174
An Example: Property Evaluation	176
Summary	178
Index	179

1

INTRODUCTION AND ACKNOWLEDGEMENTS

1.1 Introduction

Many books have been written on investment and project appraisal: most indifferent and a few excellent. All have two things in common – they are long on theory and short on application.

This book does not claim to contribute to the corpus of theory; it concentrates on evaluating a series of problems that face bankers every day and appear to have little in common. Problems covered include the financial evaluation of business strategies, both domestic and foreign; divestments; debt equity and debt bond swaps; and investment in fixed assets. The final development is a pricing model that fully reflects the liquidity and capital adequacy constraints imposed on banks by regulators in all major countries, and the model is then extended to cover relationship profitability and the gaps that need to be closed to achieve profitability targets.

It will be shown that all these problems can be realistically tackled by one basic model. The model has been applied by one of the UK clearing banks to all the areas mentioned, so that it is not a theoretical construct but a practical tool in everyday use.

The real world is far more complex than that portrayed in the theorists' models, yet such problems have been successfully handled. The use of mathematics is eschewed, apart from the occasional use of the most elementary algebra, not out of benign regard for the reader but due to the writer's own mental atrophy. All that is required is a little book-keeping and an elementary knowledge of discounted cashflow analysis.

While the basic model was developed within the context of a banking environment, it is directly relevant for all financial institutions subject to regulatory control. Company treasurers and others dealing with such institutions will wish to know how they develop rational pricing policies, while the methodologies developed will be of direct relevance to those financial analysts and investment managers concerned with the financial sector. The sections covering debt equity and debt bond swaps will be of interest to the authorities in debt-rescheduling countries, as well as the officials of the international institutions concerned. Regulators of financial institutions should find the insights offered of great assistance in understanding the institutitions they oversee.

The book is entirely self-contained. Traditional discounted cashflow (DCF) analysis is covered in the next four chapters. The rest of the book shows how DCF can be developed to solve a whole range of investment decisions within a banking context.

1.2 Acknowledgements

Particular thanks are due to my colleague Bob Moore. He displayed much patience in listening to tentative ideas and on many occasions his insight greatly speeded developments. Much is owed to Geoffrey Shields, who initiated the project and created the environment and stimulus that made it possible. I would also like to thank Jennifer Dharmawardene, and especially Debbie Keeley, for the most onerous task of all – typing the manuscript. Finally, and perhaps most importantly, thanks must go to Len Kingshott, who, when he was Director of International Banking, made me a proposal that I tried to, but in the end could not, refuse.

Over the course of a working life I have consulted academic and other published sources, but in the end I have learnt far more from doing the job and from colleagues. Nevertheless, before starting this project, I had not worked in the field for many years, and over those years major advances were made in financial theory, particularly the Capital Asset Pricing Model (CAPM). No less important was the work of proselytisers who made this work accessible to those outside academic circles. I have made liberal use of the Brierly and Myers' exposition of the CAPM in their book *Principles of Corporate Finance* (2nd edition), though I am far from sure that they would accept my interpretation in the model.

Apart from Brierly and Myers, the only other sources I have consulted have been official publications outlining the new approach regulators are taking to capital adequacy. This does not reflect a disdain for other people's work, merely the current exigencies of a working life.

Finally, it is important to make disclaimers. The methodology developed has been widely applied to various situations, but any views expressed are ultimately my own and do not necessarily reflect those of the institution I work for.

BRIAN PIZZALA

PART ONE

2

BASICS OF DISCOUNTED CASHFLOW ANALYSIS

2.1 Measuring Profitability

It is self-evident that a measure of relative profitability is needed to rank projects and other business activities. Without such a measure scarce resources could not be most profitably allocated to meet competing demands, and the business would not operate in the best interests of its owners or indeed the economy as a whole.

Very broadly, resources can be put into two groups: those with only a current time dimension and those with a future time dimension. The costs of raw materials fall into the first category. The amounts purchased can be changed at very short notice, so that their costs only need to be recovered out of current revenue. On the other hand, expenditure on fixed assets or premises can only be recouped over a number of years, sometimes several decades. Any meaningful profitability measure therefore must be able to cope with both time dimensions.

2.2 Accounting Data

The accountant's measure of capital employed attempts, but fails, to cope with these two aspects of time. Accountants may depreciate fixed assets over their putative economic lives, e.g. a machine costing £10m, with an expected life of 10 years, could be written off, or depreciated, at £1m a year. Alternatively, the asset may be depreciated on a declining balance basis, e.g. each year depreciation may be charged at, say, 20 per cent on the asset's net, or depreciated, book value. See Table 2.1.

Several points about the table need noting. Firstly net, or depreciated, asset values are shown at the end of each year, i.e. the asset would only be worth £10m at the start of year 1.

In the declining balance example 20 per cent of the initial £10m is

TABLE 2.1 Depreciation Methods Compared (£m)

| End of year | Straight line ||| Declining balance at 20 per cent |||
	Annual charge	Cumulative charge	Net asset value	Annual charge	Cumulative charge	Net asset value
1	1.0	1.0	9.0	2.0	2.0	8.0
2	1.0	2.0	8.0	1.6	3.6	6.4
3	1.0	3.0	7.0	1.3	4.9	5.1
4	1.0	4.0	6.0	1.0	5.9	4.1
5	1.0	5.0	5.0	0.8	6.7	3.3
6	1.0	6.0	4.0	0.7	7.4	2.6
7	1.0	7.0	3.0	0.5	7.9	2.1
8	1.0	8.0	2.0	0.4	8.3	1.7
9	1.0	9.0	1.0	0.4	8.7	1.3
10	1.0	10.0	–	1.3	10.0	–

written off in year 1; at the end of the year the charge of £2m is deducted from the £10m to obtain a net asset value of £8m. Likewise during year 2 the depreciation charge is 20 per cent of £8m, or £1.6m. Thus at the end of year 2 the asset is written down to £6.4m. This process continues until year 9, when at year end the asset is written down to £1.3m. If the asset is to be fully written off at the end of year 10, the depreciation change in that year must be £1.3m, not 20 per cent of £1.3m.

The rate of profitability is then measured by taking revenues less all costs, including the annual depreciation charge, divided by net asset values. However, it is clear that the annual depreciation charges, which have been conventionally calculated, are arbitrary in nature. The consequent net asset values cannot reflect the true economic or financial worth of the asset, which depends on the future profits it helps generate. Later it will be shown how a true or economic measure of depreciation can be calculated.

2.3 The Time Dimension

Even if the depreciation and net asset value problem could be ignored, the time dimension problem would remain. An example is used to illustrate this (Table 2.2).

Basics of Discounted Cashflow Analysis

TABLE 2.2

End of year	Investment 1 return on capital (%)	Investment 2 return on capital (%)
1	15.0	19.0
2	15.0	18.0
3	15.0	17.0
4	15.0	16.0
5	15.0	15.0
6	15.0	14.0
7	15.0	13.0
8	15.0	12.0
9	15.0	11.0
10	15.0	10.0
Average	15.0	14.5

There may be a temptation to say that investment 1 in Table 2.2 is best, since its average return over the 10 years is the highest, but a little reflection shows that this conclusion could be wrong. For the first 4 years investment 2 has a higher return. These surpluses relative to 1's profits could be invested elsewhere, and when this is allowed for, investment 2 could turn out better. The problem is how to derive an appropriate measure.

2.4 Present Value

The time dimension of the resource allocation problem is dealt with by turning to the theory of compound interest. The basic idea is very simple. Assume £1000 is available to invest at 10 per cent over 2 years. At the end of the year the investment is worth £1100. If the £1100 is reinvested for another year at 10 per cent, it is worth £1210 at the end of year 2.

In other words, £1000 invested for 2 years at 10 per cent compound is worth £1210 when 2 years are up. This statement can just as readily be put back-to-front by saying that £1210 2 years hence has, when the interest rate is 10 per cent, a current or present value of £1000. An investor seeking a return of 10 per cent is indifferent between £1000 now or £1210 2 years hence. He can wait 2 years for his money, or be given

[7]

FINANCIAL DECISION-MAKING

£1000, which he invests at 10 per cent to get £1210 in 2 years. This is another reason for saying that £1210 2 years hence has a present value of £1000 to this investor.

The point can be put more formally, and in a manner that makes analysis simpler. The growth in the £1000 invested over 2 years can be written:

$$£1210 = £1000 \times 1.1 \times 1.1$$
$$= £1000 \times 1.1^2$$

The term 1.1^2 is a shorthand way of writing 1.1 multiplied by itself. Generalising, 1.1 multiplied by itself n times is written 1.1^n. Thus £1000 invested at a compound rate of 10 per cent over 10 years could be written:

$$£1000 \times 1.1^{10}$$

Ten years hence this sum also has a present value of £1000 to the investor seeking a 10 per cent return. The present value (PV) of £1000 could be written:

$$PV = £1000 = \frac{£1000 \times 1.1^{10}}{1.1^{10}}$$

In obtaining the present value, the amount received 10 years hence has been divided by 1.1^{10}. Using the language of DCF analysis, the sum to be received 10 years hence has been discounted at 10 per cent over 10 years.

The ideas of present value and discounting have been introduced, but progress has been modest, for only the present value of a single future sum has been defined. It is obviously necessary to define the present value of a stream of future incomes.

Consider an initial investment of £1000 which yields 10 per cent over 5 years. The positive cashflows, including the final repayment of principal, are shown in Table 2.3.

TABLE 2.3 Cash Generated by Investment Yielding 10 per cent

End of year	Interest	Principal	Total cash received
1	100.0		100.0
2	100.0		100.0
3	100.0		100.0
4	100.0		100.0
5	100.0	1000.0	1100.0

Basics of Discounted Cashflow Analysis

A £1000 investment which yields 10 per cent every year should, if the investor is looking for a 10 per cent return, be worth £1000 to that investor today. In other words, such an investment should have a present value of £1000. This is confirmed by discounting the annual cash sums received at 10 per cent (see Table 2.4).

TABLE 2.4 Discounting an Investment Yielding 10 per cent at 10 per cent

End of year	Total cash received	Discounted cash sums	Equals	Equals
1	100	$100/1.1$	100/1.1000	90.9091
2	100	$100/1.1^2$	100/1.2100	82.6446
3	100	$100/1.1^3$	100/1.3310	75.1315
4	100	$100/1.1^4$	100/1.4641	68.3013
5	1100	$1100/1.1^5$	1100/1.6105	683.0135
Total	1500			1000.0000

Thus the sum of the discounted cashflows equals £1000, as expected. This result can be confirmed by using any other rate of interest, e.g. if a £1000 investment yields only 8 per cent, but this is all the investor looks for, such an investment should, as far as that investor is concerned, have a present value of £1000. See Table 2.5.

TABLE 2.5 Discounting an Investment Yielding 8 per cent at 8 per cent

End of year	Total cash received	Discounted cash sums	Equals	Equals
1	80	$80/1.08$	80/1.0800	74.0741
2	80	$80/1.08^2$	80/1.1664	68.5871
3	80	$80/1.08^3$	80/1.2597	63.5066
4	80	$80/1.08^4$	80/1.3605	58.8024
5	1080	$1080/1.08^5$	1080/1.4693	735.0298
Total	1400			1000.0000

2.5 Net Present Value

So far we have only considered cases where one initial and equal amount has been invested. Competing investment projects will have different initial levels of investment, and in major projects the investment will also run over several years. Therefore a measure that takes account of the varied nature of projects is needed. This is done by converting present values to net present values (NPVs).

In the examples shown in Tables 2.4 and 2.5 the present value in both cases is £1000. The net present value is calculated by treating the initial £1000 investment as a negative cashflow. When this is done, the net present value in both cases becomes zero.

More generally a zero net present value shows that a project breaks even, i.e. it just earns the required rate of interest. A negative net present value means the project is not worthwhile, as it does not earn the required rate of interest or required rate of return. A project with a positive net present value earns more than the required return.

2.6 An Example

Table 2.2 illustrated the problem of deciding which of two investments was best; the problem can now be solved by considering net present values. In both cases assume that the initial investment is £1000 and that investment 1 earns 15 per cent in each of the 10 years. In case 2 assume that the returns earned each year are those shown in Table 2.2. In both cases it is further assumed that the initial investment is recouped at the end of year 10. With these assumptions the cashflows and net present values are shown in Table 2.6. Hence on discounting at 10 per cent project 2 has a higher net present value, even though its average return is less than project 1's.

If the investor had been seeking a 15 per cent return, then investment 1 would break even, and its NPV would have been zero. Similarly, had project 2's cashflows been discounted at 15.66 per cent, its net present value would have been zero. Unfortunately there is no simple formula for deriving the 15.66 per cent; it is found by trial and error using a standard PC programme. Investment 1 therefore generates a return of 15 per cent, while investment 2's return is 15.66 per cent, compared with 15 per cent and 14.5 per cent respectively derived from the average accounting returns shown in Table 2.2.

Basics of Discounted Cashflow Analysis

TABLE 2.6 Comparison of Net Present Values at 10 per cent

End of year	Cash-flows	Project 1 Discounted cash sums	Equals	Cash-flows	Project 2 Discounted cashflows	Equals
0	(1000)	(1000.00)	(1000.0000)	(1000)	(1000)	(1000.0000)
1	150	150/1.1	136.3636	190	190/1.1	172.7273
2	150	$150/1.1^2$	123.9669	180	$180/1.1^2$	148.7603
3	150	$150/1.1^3$	112.6972	170	$170/1.1^3$	127.7235
4	150	$150/1.1^4$	102.4520	160	$160/1.1^4$	109.2822
5	150	$150/1.1^5$	93.1382	150	$150/1.1^5$	93.1382
6	150	$150/1.1^6$	84.6711	140	$140/1.1^6$	79.0264
7	150	$150/1.1^7$	76.9737	130	$130/1.1^7$	66.7106
8	150	$150/1.1^8$	69.9761	120	$120/1.1^8$	55.9809
9	150	$150/1.1^9$	63.6146	110	$110/1.1^7$	46.6507
10	1150	$1150/1.1^{10}$	443.3748	1100	$1100/1.1^{10}$	424.0976
NPV			307.2284			324.0976

2.7 A Hidden Assumption

The idea of present value was introduced via the use of compound interest, and by noting that if an investor can earn 10 per cent on his funds, he is indifferent between £121 2 years hence and £100 today. Likewise he is indifferent between an investment yielding £10 each year (provided he gets his principal back) and £100 today. The present value of both investments is £100, and both have a net present value of zero.

The idea was then generalised by saying that any income stream or series of cashflows could be discounted at the return the investor was seeking. An illustration was given in Table 2.6; another example is shown in Table 2.7.

In this case the initial investment of £100 yields £6 at the end of year 1, and £14.4 at the end of year 2, when the principal is also repaid. Discounting at 10 per cent gives a NPV of zero, apparently showing that the investment gives a return of exactly 10 per cent. This conclusion is correct if, and only if, the £6 earned at the end of year 1 can be reinvested at 10 per cent during year 2.

The investment can only earn a true interest rate of 10 per cent if at the end of year 2 the investor ends up with £121, i.e. a compound return of 10 per cent over 2 years. If the £6 earned at the end of year 1 is invested

[11]

FINANCIAL DECISION-MAKING

TABLE 2.7   NPV of an Irregular Cashflow

End of year	Earnings	Principal	Total cash	Discounted cash	Equals
0	–	(100.0)	(100.0)	(100.0)	(100.000000)
1	6.0		6.0	6.0/1.1	5.454545
2	14.4	100.0	114.4	114.4/1.1^2	94.545455
NPV					0.000000

and earns 10 per cent, it yields £6.6 a year later. At the end of year 2 the investor ends up with exactly £121, i.e. £6.6 + £114.4. Had the £6 been invested at any rate other than 10 per cent, the investor would not have ended up with exactly £121 after 2 years.

2.8   The True Rate of Return

The true return on a project or investment is that rate of interest which generates a zero NPV – in DCF analysis called the internal rate of return (IRR). Thus, simply by definition, when a project is discounted at its true or internal rate of return, its NPV is zero. However, it is important to bear in mind that the concept is somewhat artificial. Section 2.7 showed that an implicit assumption of DCF analysis is that the cashflows in any year can be reinvested at exactly the required return or discount rate, but in practice the IRR will only occasionally approximate to the return sought by investors. This is one reason why NPV is a sounder criterion than the IRR. Nevertheless, provided the appropriate caveat is borne in mind, the IRR does give a reasonable and often useful guide to a project's rate of profitability.

2.9   Economic Depreciation

Deriving a true economic measure of depreciation demonstrates the arbitrary nature of conventional or accounting measures. At the same time it provides a simultaneous example of DCF and IRR analysis, and so facilitates understanding of the concepts, which are also of importance to the idea of the weighted cost of capital (introduced in Chapter 5).

Basics of Discounted Cashflow Analysis

The value of an asset shown in a company's balance sheet is meant to reflect its true or economic worth. Property values quite often approximate to this ideal, at least when they are revalued to reflect market conditions, but the valuation of other fixed assets is quite arbitrary. In principle, however, it is possible to calculate the changing economic worth of an asset and the consequent depreciation charges.

An asset's economic worth is the discounted value of its future earnings. At the same time the total of all depreciation charges must add up to the original cost of the asset. The latter requirement can be satisfied by using the asset's IRR, which guarantees a zero NPV, and so a 100 per cent write-off of the asset's purchase price. The details are illustrated in Table 2.8.

TABLE 2.8 Economic Depreciation Discounting at 15 per cent

End of year	Cash-flow	NPV of remaining cashflows	Depreciation	Profit after depreciation	Rate of profit (%)
0	(1000.0)	0.0			
1	450.0	1000.0	300.0	150.0	15.0
2	355.0	700.0	250.0	105.0	15.0
3	267.5	450.0	200.0	67.5	15.0
4	187.5	250.0	150.0	37.5	15.0
5	115.0	100.0	100.0	15.0	15.0

In this project there is an initial capital expenditure of £1000. A year later £450 of cash is generated, and a year after that £355. Finally, 5 years after the investment, only £115 is obtained. If the project's cashflows are discounted at 15 per cent, its net present value is zero. This value is the first entry in the third column. Discounting all the positive cashflows at 15 per cent gives a value of £1000, which is the project's present value. Looked at from another perspective, it is the economic worth of the project viewed at the start of year 1 immediately after the £1000 has been spent.

Likewise the economic worth of the project can be calculated from the beginning of year 2. All the cash inflows from £355 to £155 are discounted at 15 per cent. The value of these discounted cashflows is £700. This process can be undertaken each year until the beginning of year 5 is reached. At this point the value of the project is £115/1.15, or £100, the final value shown in column 3.

This sequence of discounted cashflows represents the true economic

FINANCIAL DECISION-MAKING

worth of the asset over each of the remaining years of its life. Strictly, therefore, they should represent the asset's net book worth each year. Depreciation is the diminution of the asset's value from one year to the next. Thus in year 2 the depreciation charge is £250: the difference between £700 and £450, the asset's value in years 2 and 3 respectively.

The penultimate column shows the profit, or cashflow, after deduction of that year's depreciation charge. Hence year 1's profit after depreciation is £450 less £300, that is £150.

Finally the rate of profit is shown. It is profit after depreciation divided by the asset's net book value, remembering that the latter is the discounted value of the remaining cashflows. In year 3, for example, the rate of profit is:

$$\frac{(267.5 - 200.0)}{450} \times 100 = 15 \text{ per cent}$$

Hence in every year the rate of profit equals the asset's true or internal rate of return, which is exactly what is required of any meaningful measure of net asset values and depreciation. With an economic measure of an asset's net worth economically valid depreciation charges can be derived. Therefore the earlier contention that conventional depreciation charges are arbitrary is confirmed, and the superiority of the DCF approach is unambiguously demonstrated.

3

SHAREHOLDER VALUE

3.1 Rationale

The overriding objective of a business is to maximise profits on behalf of its owners. Since nearly all businesses are incorporated as limited companies, this means maximising profits on behalf of shareholders. Investment projects generate profits over many years, but maximisation of short-term profitability may impinge upon longer-term profits; high prices and profits now will cause a loss of future sales which may result in future profits being less than they might have been.

Maximising profits in the short term therefore may not be in the best long-term financial interest of shareholders. In fact their financial well-being is best served if the present value of their company's future earnings is maximised. This is equivalent to maximising the net present values of the companies they own, and should ultimately be reflected in the market value of their shares. The maximisation of shareholder wealth or value also enables the shareholder to maximise his cash holdings by selling his shares at the highest market value possible.

Maximisation of shareholder value is currently one of the major concepts and tools of consultants and financial analysts, and holds great sway with much of the business community. Often it takes on the character of a revealed metaphysical truth, yet it is nothing more than long-term, as opposed to short-term, profit maximisation rediscovered and repackaged. As all economic textbooks demonstrate, profit maximisation only generates maximum benefit for the whole community in an effectively competitive environment. Efficient resource allocation in a fully competitive economy is one of the main requirements of the capitalist system. Monopoly or oligopolistic pricing, whether explicit or implicit, is recognised to be against the public interest; but governments commit large resources attempting to circumvent market exploitation by groups of companies, and thereby deliberately, and rightly, frustrate maximisation of shareholder value.

FINANCIAL DECISION-MAKING

This should not deter anyone from the conscientious pursuit of corporate objectives. Nevertheless those employing current business philosophies should be aware of their fundamental shortcomings, whatever advantages they bring to the company's shareholders. With this caveat made, the rest of the chapter considers a number of topics relevant to the financial analysis of companies and hence shareholder value. They are all topics that are often misunderstood within the business community. Their clarification should be an important contribution to the understanding of financial decision-making and resource allocation.

3.2 Earnings and Dividends Compared

In this section the relation between earnings, dividends, net present value and shareholder value is explored. An important result, frequently used in financial analysis to judge the efficiency of companies, is thereby derived.

On the basis of Chapter 2's analysis the following statements would seem mutually consistent. A bank's audited net worth or book value is £1bn, the market value of its shares is £1bn, earnings are 15 per cent of net worth or £150m, and the bank's shareholders seek a 15 per cent return. See Table 3.1.

TABLE 3.1 Discounted Earnings at 15 per cent: No Retentions (£m)

End of year	Cashflows	Discounted cashflows	Equals
0	(1000.0)	(1000.0)	(1000.0000)
1	150.0	150/1.15	130.4348
2	150.0	$150/1.15^2$	113.4216
3	150.0	$150/1.15^3$	98.6274
4	150.0	$150/1.15^4$	85.7630
5	1150.0	$1150/1.15^5$	571.7532
NPV			0.0000

Since the market value of the shares is £1bn, the cost to shareholders of owning the bank is also £1bn, as any individual shareholder has the option of selling his shares at market value. Annual earnings equal 15 per cent of book value, or £150m a year. At the end of year 5 it is assumed that

[16]

Shareholder Value

the shareholders receive £1150m, i.e. year 5's earnings plus the book value of the bank.

However, since the market value and the book value are assumed to remain at £1bn throughout the 5 years, it follows that all earnings must have been distributed as dividends. Had any earnings been retained, then the bank's book value would have increased, and its market value, it is hoped, by the same amount. Shareholders have in effect invested £1bn in a bank paying annual dividends of £150m. At the end of 5 years they sell their shares for £1bn as well as receiving dividends of £150m. Their investment provides an IRR of 15 per cent, and if they seek a 15 per cent return on their investment, its NPV must be zero.

This example demonstrates the commonly held view that the market value of a company's shares equals its accounting book value when its profits in relation to its book value equal the return shareholders seek.

Thus shares provide two sources of income or cash for shareholders: dividends and share sale proceeds. Therefore in judging whether or not to buy shares the investor must take a view on dividends and the eventual sale price, in relation to his initial investment. Thus the NPV of a share purchase is the discounted stream of dividends, plus the discounted value of the revenue from selling the shares, less their initial cost.

It is now possible to show that even when profits are retained, the present value of the shareholders' income stream will equal the company's book value when earnings, as a percentage of book value, equal the return shareholders seek. In a rational market share prices will equal the present value of the income stream received by shareholders. Hence the previous conclusion holds whatever a company's retention policy.

TABLE 3.2 Discounted Earnings at 15 per cent: Two-Thirds Retention (£m)

End of year	Earnings	Dividends	Retentions	Book value	Shareholders' cashflow	Discounted cashflow
0	–	–	–	1000.000		
1	150.000	50.000	100.000	1100.000	50.000	43.4783
2	165.000	55.000	110.000	1210.000	55.000	41.5879
3	181.500	60.500	121.000	1331.000	60.500	39.7797
4	199.650	66.550	133.100	1464.100	66.550	38.0502
5	219.615	73.205	146.410	1610.510	1683.715	837.1039
						1000.0000

FINANCIAL DECISION-MAKING

In Table 3.2 the initial book value is £1bn. In year 1 earnings at 15 per cent are £150m, one third of earnings (i.e. £50m) is paid as dividends and retentions are £100m. At the end of year 1 therefore book value is £1100m.

Remember earnings are specified to be 15 per cent of book value throughout the 5 years, so that earnings at the end of year 2 are £165m, or 15 per cent of £1100m. At one third of earnings year 2 dividends are £55m and retentions £110m. On the addition of retained earnings of £110m to the end of year 1's book value of £1100m, book value becomes £1210m at the end of year 2. This process carries on until the end of year 5, when the investors receive dividends of £73.205m, and sell the shares for their book value of £1610.51m.

In summary, shareholders receive an initial dividend of £50m. Owing to retentions and a constant return of 15 per cent, dividends grow at 10 per cent a year for the next 4 years, and in the final year shareholders receive their dividend and sell their shares at book value. The cash inflows are shown in the penultimate column, and their discounted values in the final column. As expected, the latter add up to £1bn. Therefore, provided the sale value of the shares equals the terminal book value, the shares at the beginning of year 1 are worth £1bn.

In addition these examples show that under the DCF criterion the shareholder is indifferent between all earnings being paid out in dividends and any level of retentions, provided the rate of earnings equals the return shareholders' require and the shares can eventually be sold for book value. Indeed in the extreme case when all profits are retained, and the shares are sold at the end of year 5 for book value, the NPV is still zero:

$$\text{NPV} = (\pounds 1\text{bn}) + \frac{\pounds 1\text{bn} \times 1.15^5}{1.15^5} = 0$$

3.3 Retained Profits v Dividends

The previous section showed that a shareholder is indifferent between dividends and retained profits, provided (i) the company is earning exactly the return sought by shareholders and (ii) the terminal market value of the shares equals book value.

Neither assumption is realistic. If the company earns more than the return sought by the shareholder, then all earnings should be retained. For example, the shareholder may seek 15 per cent and the company

Shareholder Value

earn 20 per cent, or 5 percentage points more than the shareholder can earn elsewhere. The company is clearly a more remunerative investment, provided the shareholder can purchase its shares at book value. Two examples demonstrate the point:

$$\text{NPV} = (\pounds1000\text{m}) + \frac{\pounds200\text{m}}{1.15} + \frac{\pounds200\text{m}}{1.15^2} + \frac{\pounds1200\text{m}}{1.15^3} \cdots \cdots \quad (3.1)$$
$$= \pounds114.16\text{m}$$

$$\text{NPV} = (\pounds1000\text{m}) + \frac{0}{1.15} + \frac{0}{1.15^2} + \frac{\pounds1000\text{m} \, 1.2^3}{1.15^3} \cdots \cdots \quad (3.2)$$
$$= \pounds136.19\text{m}$$

Equation 3.1 assumes that all earnings are paid out in dividends, and gives a NPV of 114.16; no dividends are paid in equation 3.2, and the shares are sold at book value at the end of year 3, to give an NPV of 136.19. In both examples investors earn a surplus, and competitive pressures will eradicate such surpluses as investors bid up share prices to participate in the surplus. In practice the value of the shares will range between £1114.2m and £1136.2m, depending upon anticipated profit retentions. Whatever the retention policy, it is clear that the market value of the shares will exceed the company's book value of £1000m, and the opposite when the company cannot earn 15 per cent.

Shareholders' wealth or value is at its highest when the value of their shares is maximised. Clearly the higher the rate of return earned by a company, the greater the value of its shares. From this it is often concluded that shareholder value is maximised when a company maximises the return earned on its net book value. Many companies earn a lesser rate of profit than the return sought by their shareholders, and in these circumstances shareholder interests are best served by the maximum dividend possible. Indeed the company should really be run down so that its funds can be more usefully deployed elsewhere in the economy.

3.4 Average and Marginal Earnings Compared

The analysis in the previous section appeared to conclude that shareholder wealth or value is at its highest when companies maximise the rate of return earned. This, however, is to misconceive the nature of an enterprise. The models used so far treat the company as if it were a single project, but in reality most companies consist of a whole range of projects and disparate business activities. Indeed the whole rationale of project apraisal is to determine which of these disparate activities the business should commit its funds to. It is very likely that in many circumstances the best interests of the shareholders are served by deliberately lowering their company's average rate of profitability.

A single business company with a book value of £500m may earn 30 per cent or £150m a year. If its shareholders seek a 15 per cent return, the market value of its shares will be substantially in excess of its book value. An opportunity may occur to buy another business which, at the purchase price of £250m, will yield the company only 20 per cent. The company's chief financial officer advises the board not to buy the business, since it will dilute its earnings from 30 per cent to just over 26.7 per cent, that is:

$$\frac{£500m \times 0.30 + £250m \times 0.20}{(£500m + £250m)} = 0.267$$

The board agrees. In the unlikely event that the shareholders get wind of this decision they should ask the board to reconsider it. The company has given up a golden opportunity to earn its shareholders a surplus return of 5 per cent – 20 per cent against their required 15 per cent. Annual surplus profits of £12.5m have been cast aside. In present value terms the shareholders have lost out by £83.3m, i.e. £12.5m discounted at 15 per cent in perpetuity.

It is possible that the company does not have sufficient funds for the investment, and that some of the shareholders do not wish to contribute towards the £250m. Nevertheless the money can still be raised without harming the existing shareholders' interests. Profits before the purchase amount to £150m, and existing shareholders must still obtain this amount after the acquisition. As total profits after acquisition are £200m, they must own 150/200 or 75 per cent of the company. If the current number of shares is 750m, then the project can be equitably financed by issuing 250 million £1 shares to new shareholders. Any existing shareholder can also take up these shares and earn 20 per cent on his investment while still earning 30 per cent on his other shares.

The lesson is clear – any project or investment that earns at least 15 per cent should be undertaken. Its impact on the average rate of profitability, so-called dilution, is irrelevant.

3.5 Real and Nominal Returns

The world is an inflationary one. It might be possible to ignore inflation if it were both low and constant, but even in OECD countries the latter stipulation is untrue, and in a number of these countries inflation has exceeded 10 per cent a year on occasions. Variable and even modest inflation results in all kinds of distortions. An asset yielding 10 per cent p.a. provides the investor with no real benefit if inflation is 10 per cent p.a., since the investor's purchasing power is unchanged a year after his investment. The purchasing power of the asset plus its 10 per cent interest is unchanged. Had there been no inflation, purchasing power would have increased 10 per cent – the asset's yield. With inflation at 10 per cent the asset is said to yield a zero real rate of return.

More generally, but somewhat loosely, the real rate of return is often defined as the actual or nominal rate of interest less the rate of inflation, i.e. with 10 per cent interest and 5 per cent inflation the real rate of return is said to be 5 per cent. Strictly this is only an approximation. If someone's income increases 20 per cent over a year from an initial £20,000, it will become £20,000 × 1.20. If prices in general increase 20 per cent, his real income remains unchanged, i.e.:

$$\frac{£20,000 \times 1.2}{1.2} = £20,000$$

Had prices only increased 10 per cent, his real income would be:

$$\frac{£20,000 \times 1.2}{1.1} = £20,000 \times 1.0909$$

Real income has not increased 10 per cent but only 9.09 per cent, i.e.:

$$(1.0909-1) \times 100, \text{ where } 1.0909 = \frac{1.2}{1.1}$$

More generally the real rate of return is defined as:

$$\frac{(1 + \text{yield})}{(1 + \text{inflation})} - 1$$

The distinction between real and/or nominal returns is crucial, since investors will only be interested in the real, not nominal, increase in their wealth. Moreover comparison of past yields with current yields will be meaningless if the inflation rates of the periods are different.

Calculating present values, as such, is a simple and mechanical procedure which is normally carried out on a calculator or standard PC program. A key factor in all DCF analysis is the interest or discount rate employed. The return it is assumed that shareholders seek can only be based on historical analysis. Past returns, as noted, will be distorted by inflation, and previous rates of inflation are unlikely to bear much relation to the inflation rate implicit in profit forecasts, so that it is necessary to estimate past shareholder returns in real terms. These real yields can then be converted to a nominal yield or target return consistent with the inflation rate built into profit forecasts.

3.6 Is the Price/Earnings Ratio Meaningful?

Financial analysts, accountants, corporate planners and others talk about various financial ratios that are used to help judge financial performance, and guide decision-making. Perhaps the most important of these ratios is the price/earnings or PE ratio, which shows the market value (MV) of a company's shares divided by post tax earnings. The PE ratio is written MV/Earnings, and its inverse, the earnings yield, is written Earnings/MV. The latter is the yield shareholders would obtain if they purchased the shares at current market values.

When the MV of shares equals the company's book value (BV), the earnings yield will equal the company's rate of profitability, i.e.:

$$\frac{\text{Earnings}}{\text{MV}} = \frac{\text{Earnings}}{\text{BV}} = \text{rate of profitability}$$

As demonstrated in sections 3.2 and 3.3, market value equals book value when the rate of profit equals the return sought by shareholders. Some analysts and consultants conclude from this that a company's rate of profitability is satisfactory when market value equals book value; quite apart from large irrational fluctuations in share prices and the arbitrary nature of book worth, it will be shown that this conclusion is still invalid. A second everyday statement is that a low earnings yield, or high PE ratio, signals the market's expectation that a company's earnings will increase. A third commonly held view is that if company A's shareholders seek a return higher than company B's earnings yield, then B is too expensive for A to acquire. These propositions are also invalid.

Shareholder Value

The second of the propositions is examined first. All companies that retain earnings will see their earnings grow, as Table 3.2 clearly illustrates. Provided that the earnings yield equals the return required, the company's book value will equal its market value and the PE ratio will remain unchanged. However, the second proposition can be appropriately restated to say a low earnings yield (and hence high PE ratio) signals a market expectation that a company's rate of profitability will increase. Equations 3.1 and 3.2 (p.19) do show that the NPV of investing in a company would increase if the future rate of profit is expected to rise. Consequently, share prices should increase. Therefore, in relation to current earnings, the earnings yield will fall and the PE ratio increase.

Once the new rate of profitability has been established, the PE ratio will stabilise. The rate at which it stabilises will depend upon various parameters, including the new rate of profitability compared to the return sought by shareholders, the proportion of earnings retained, and the shareholders' time horizon, i.e. the period over which they evaluate their investments.

A continuing increase in PE ratios, or continuing decline in the earnings yield, can only be justified if the rate of profitability is expected to go on increasing. Moreover, for the market as a whole, increased profitability expectations can only lead to an increase in PE ratios if shareholders fail to increase their required return fully in line with their expectation of greater profitability.

The reasoning above is correct on the assumptions made, but implicit assumptions are often more important than those made explicit. All the examples or models used so far contain a hidden critical caveat, which is a non-inflationary world. Once the reality of inflation is made explicit, the conclusions and notions so freely put about fall apart.

When accountants do adjust balance sheets for inflation, the rest of the world often ignores them. Only the historic cost accounts seem to be given any attention, and the book value of plant, machinery and similar fixed assets are taken from the books at their original, or historic, cost. Depreciation charges too are based on historic costs. The real worth of these assets will, however, have increased in line with inflation, so that their book value will be too low. Accountants and economists do have rules for adjusting asset values and profits for inflation. These adjustments (replacement cost accounting) increase the published value of fixed assets, but also reduce the level of published profits.

Asset values adjusted upwards for inflation will reflect their true value more reliably than historic cost accounts. Stock markets should, over a run of years, reflect the true worth of companies; on average therefore stock market valuations will be higher than the historic cost-based book values of companies. Thus even when company earnings exactly match their shareholders' requirements, market values will, owing to inflation, exceed book values. Therefore in the real world MV will not equal BV, even when the company earns the return required of it. Rather MV will tend to exceed BV.

Published earnings yield ratios therefore have a denominator that approximately reflects replacement cost valuations. In principle the numerator should be the accountant's historic cost measure of earnings, and then the earnings yield would be real yield with inflation netted out. However, as historic cost profits are used, the denominator and numerator are incompatible, and the PE and earnings yield ratios are meaningless for many companies.

Nevertheless, in spite of the incongruities, some useful information can be gleaned from these ratios. The denominator should, over a run of years, broadly reflect the replacement cost measure of a company's net worth, and the profits measure be higher than one reflecting the downward inflationary adjustments. Hence the earnings yield will overestimate the replacement-cost-based profitability rate, and so the real rate of return, and the earnings yield will underestimate the nominal return sought by shareholders.

Current (August 1988) UK PE ratios are in the region of 12:1, implying an average earnings yield of around 8.3 per cent. Given the current state of the UK economy, it is unlikely that the rate of profitability will increase much. PE ratios cannot therefore be high on this score, and it seems reasonable to conclude that shareholders in general seek a real return of less than 8 per cent.

Finally it should now be apparent that the third of the propositions is incorrect. The earnings yield cannot measure the nominal return companies earn, and no conclusions can be drawn about a company's rate of profitability in relation to the price of its shares. Consequently it is impossible to draw conclusions about the attractiveness of an acquisition on the basis of earnings yields or PE ratios.

4

COST OF EQUITY AND THE CAPITAL ASSET PRICING MODEL

4.1 Measuring Returns on Equity

4.1.1 Introduction

There are two main problem areas in DCF analysis: estimating future cashflows, and assessing the return shareholders seek, i.e. the cost of equity (COE). Discounting, as such, is merely a mechanical task that can be safely delegated to a PC. Significant errors in estimating the COE will result in compounded errors of analysis. A rate that is too high will result in under-investment and slower than optimal business expansion; not only will this frustrate maximisation of shareholder value but it will be harmful for the economy and so the whole community. When the estimated COE is too low, unprofitable schemes will be implemented and resources wasted.

In spite of its importance, measuring the COE is fraught with difficulties, and is an area of contention. Even if returns achieved by shareholders can be measured, there is no guarantee that this reflects the return they actually seek. The return obtained by shareholders is derived from the discounted value of dividends and the sale price of the shares in relation to their purchase price, the return being the discount rate which gives a zero NPV, i.e. the IRR. Observed returns to shareholders can only be based on past values of dividends and share values. Suppose however that investor preferences move away from interest-bearing instruments to equities, perhaps due to their awareness of the ravages of inflation. Interest rates will increase as the value of interest-bearing instruments fall, and the price of shares will increase, reflecting their greater attractiveness. Since equities are now more attractive, the return shareholders expect will fall in line with their increased value. Yet the measured return on equities will initially increase as the price at which they can be sold increases more than otherwise. Thus the measured

FINANCIAL DECISION-MAKING

return will increase even though shareholders now require a lesser return from their equity investments.

Quite apart from such behavioural problems, the methods available for estimating shareholder returns all have their difficulties. Such problems do not obviate the need for estimation, but they should put people on guard, so enabling them to make more informed judgements.

4.1.2 The Arithmetic Average

Much work has been done on estimating the return obtained by shareholders. Owing to the great volatility of stockmarkets, such studies are done over relatively long periods of time. For the USA the study normally quoted is that of Ibbotson and Sinquefield, which covered the period 1926 to 1981 and calculated annual returns from the Standard and Poor's Composite Index, representing a portfolio of common stocks of 500 large firms. The calculated annual return was:

$$\frac{V(n) - V(n-1) + D}{V(n-1)} \quad \quad (4.1)$$

where $V(n)$ is the value of the share price index in year n, $V(n-1)$ the value of the share price index in the prior year, and D the annual dividend.

For the whole period the average return, calculated by dividing the sum of the annual returns by 55, was 11.4 per cent p.a. or an 8.3 per cent real return on netting out inflation.

It can be shown, however, that this measure cannot in practice provide a reliable guide to the COE or the return sought by shareholders. Take as an example a company that earns 10 per cent p.a., pays all earnings in dividends, and has shareholders who are content with a 10 per cent return. Stock markets are volatile, so its share price will vary year by year, but for illustrative purposes it is assumed that in both years 0 and 4 market value equals book value of £100m. See Table 4.1.

The annual returns are calculated by means of the formula 4.1, and the arithmetic mean of the four annual returns is 12.3 per cent. Clearly this bears no relation to either the return being earned and the return sought. Using the 12.3 per cent mean would have the paradoxical result of forcing companies to seek a return higher than necessary, with obvious adverse consequences.

Cost of Equity and the Capital Asset Pricing Model

TABLE 4.1 Annual COE: Arithmetic Mean

End of year	Share price (£m)	Dividend (£m)	Annual return (%)
0	100		
1	80	10	(10.00)
2	100	10	37.50
3	120	10	30.00
4	100	10	(8.33)

4.1.3 The Geometric Mean or Income Reinvested Method

Compound interest is a geometric phenomenon, and replacing the arithmetic mean by the geometric mean should overcome the former's shortcomings. Table 4.1's data can be used to illustrate the calculation. A shareholder can buy shares at the beginning of the year, and both take his dividend and sell the shares at year end. At the end of year 1 he would have suffered a 10 per cent loss. However, repeating this exercise in the following year would give a 37.5 per cent return over the year. Over the 4 years the investor would earn, ignoring transaction costs:

$$100 \times 0.90 \times 1.375 \times 1.300 \times 0.9167$$

to give a cumulative return of 47.5 per cent, or a compounded rate of return of 10.2 per cent. In other words, £100m invested for 4 years at 10.2 per cent compound gives £147.5m at the end of year 4. The estimated return is too high, though the error is very small. In practice the error can be large and either positive or negative, as shown in Tables 4.2a and b.

Thus the cumulative return from Table 4.2a is:

$$100 \times 0.6000 \times 1.7000 \times 1.4667 = £149.6m$$

to give a compound interest rate, or geometric average of 14.3 per cent.

The cumulative return from Table 4.2b is:

$$100 \times 1.60 \times 0.90 \times 0.88 = £126.7m$$

to give a geometric average of 8.2 per cent. Tables 4.2 (a) and 4.2 (b) illustrate a general proposition. During periods when share prices move

TABLE 4.2a Average Cost of Equity: Geometric Mean (Case A)

End of year	Share price (£m)	Dividend (£m)	Annual return (%)
0	100		
1	50	10	(40.00)
2	75	10	70.00
3	100	10	46.67

TABLE 4.2b Average Cost of Equity: Geometric mean (Case B)

End of year	Share price (£m)	Dividend (£m)	Annual return (%)
0	100		
1	150	10	60.00
2	125	10	(10.00)
3	100	10	(12.00)

below trend, the geometric mean overestimates the COE, and when share prices move above trend, it underestimates them, provided in both cases that the price starts at about and ends at about trend levels. The geometric mean estimate is also known as the 'income reinvested method'.

Neither of the previous methods uses the income stream actually received by shareholders. When this is done, the examples given in Tables 4.1 and 4.2 show that the COE is correctly estimated by the IRR. But even this calculation only works if the start and end values of the index are more or less on trend. Owing to the difficulties of determining trend value the next two sections examine alternative measures.

4.2 UK Cost of Equity: an Alternative Approach

In the UK the pioneering work on estimating the COE was undertaken by Merrett and Sykes. The most comprehensive recent work is that by Barclays de Zoete Wedd in their Equity-Gilt study, which covers combinations of time periods from December 1918 to December 1986. The real returns on equities and gilts are considered, and some of their results are shown in Table 4.3. They are based on the reinvestment or geometric mean method, and the appropriate caveats should be borne in mind.

Cost of Equity and the Capital Asset Pricing Model

TABLE 4.3   Real Return on UK Equities and Gifts

Period	Equities	Gilts	Differential
	Annual average returns (%)		
1918–86	7.3	0.9	6.4
1950–86	7.3	(0.9)	8.2
1960–86	5.2	0.1	5.1
1970–86	6.5	1.1	5.4
1975–86	12.0	5.4	6.6
1980–86	17.1	8.7	8.4

Until the period 1970 to 1986 the range of equity yields was moderate, but more recently real returns have shot up. Does this mean that there has been a fundamental change in equity markets and shareholder expectations? More detailed analyses suggest not. During the mid-1970s equity markets suffered a severe bear phase, and even by 1980 equities were still slightly below trend. Subsequently the market went through a strong bull period, when equity returns, as measured, were dominated by capital gains, with dividends making a relatively limited contribution. Had the 10 year period 1972–82 been taken, the average real return would have been a negative 1.5 per cent, because 1972 was a peak year while 1982 was nearer to trend. Over this period capital losses dominated the situation and more than offset the benefit of dividends.

Over any arbitrary time period it is most unlikely that share-price movements and returns will reflect both company earnings and shareholder requirements. From about 1950 to 1970 share prices exhibited a fairly steady upward movement of just over 7 per cent p.a., dividend yields fluctuated minimally around 5 per cent p.a., yet earnings yields fell by over half from the mid-1950s. It was only possible to maintain dividends in relation to market value by the retention of an ever-decreasing proportion of profits. Thus the fairly steady return being achieved by shareholders bore no relation to the underlying earning capacity of companies. Similarly during the 1980s share prices increased far faster than the underlying recovery in company profitability.

Nevertheless, historic data does give clues to the return that satisfies shareholders; in the long run there has been relative consistency in dividend yields of around 5 per cent. Apart from speculators, shareholders, by the very nature of their investments, take a long view, which means that their return will be primarily determined by dividends received. Share prices cannot continuously grow faster than the economy as a whole. If they did, shareholders would earn an ever-increasing share of the national income, eventually taking the lot. Broadly, this means that on average and over long periods dividends cannot grow at more than around 3 per cent a year in real terms. An initial return of 5 per cent subsequently growing at 3 per cent p.a. in real terms actually provides an 8 per cent annual real return.

It seems reasonable to conclude that UK shareholders are happy with a real return of around 8 per cent. For what it's worth, this is only marginally higher than the return actually received in all but the last decade and a half, and, as demonstrated, these later returns were artificially high. Moreover, 14 months after the October 1987 crash dividend yields were still below 5 per cent. In the economic circumstances of that time it was not reasonable to expect the real rate of profitability to increase. If anything, the opposite was more likely to be the case over the following few years.

At the end of Chapter 3 the earnings yield was given a new and correct interpretation. It was shown that in equilibrium conditions the earnings yield would underestimate the real return sought by shareholders. Fourteen months after the crash market yield suggested a real requirement of well under 8 per cent. Only if share prices had been grossly overvalued, or shareholders had expected a steep increase in the real returns earned by companies, would the conclusion be invalid. However, neither of these possibilities was particularly plausible.

4.3 The Capital Asset Pricing Model

4.3.1 *Theoretical Framework*

The capital asset pricing model (CAPM) is an attempt to solve two problems simultaneously. It addresses the problem of estimating the economy-wide, or average, cost of equity, while looking at company, or at least sector, specific COEs. The theory suggests that the COE varies between different types of business activity, increasing with the relative riskiness of the sector.

Risk in this context has a technical definition rather than the everyday usage of the term. Thus a particular company may have a 10 per cent probability of going bankrupt, and another may, for all practical purposes, have a zero probability of failure. Yet in the context of the CAPM both companies could be subject to exactly the same degree of risk.

In the CAPM risk is not defined as the likelihood, or expected value, of

Cost of Equity and the Capital Asset Pricing Model

forecast profits; it is defined as the variability of profits, or more strictly the variability of the return on equities, about their expected rate. The variability in returns is broken into two components: a so-called company-specific risk and a company systematic risk. Only the latter is considered relevant. Over a run of years share prices in general exhibit great variability. In the CAPM model annual returns are measured by the method defined by formula 4.1. This means that the measured return is dominated by movements in share-price indices from one period to the next, as dividend payments generally tend to grow at a fairly steady pace. Hence returns, as defined, show great variability.

Individual share prices are also very variable, often more so than the market in general. A company's specific risk, or variability, is that aspect of the volatility of the return on its shares that is not correlated with movements in general equity returns. Such volatility is treated as entirely random. By holding a portfolio of equities, company specific risks can be eliminated, as above-average returns will be more or less offset by below-average returns. Since shareholders can invest in a portfolio, they can, if they wish, virtually eliminate company-specific risks. Hence such risks or volatility can be ignored.

Systematic risk is another matter. To an extent most individual share prices will be correlated to market prices in general. The economic, political and other factors that increase share prices, profits and dividends for the whole market will to a degree have the same impact on individual shares; likewise when market returns suffer. Thus there will always be some, but not perfect, correlation between the return on shares in general and the return on any particular equity. This correlation is the systematic risk that pertains to an individual company's shares.

As a matter of convenience the variability of the return on all equities is set at one. More formally the variability of the total market return is said to have a Beta = 1. The variability of the whole equity market sets one benchmark, but another is required – the putative risk-free rate of interest, which means an interest rate that is guaranteed under all conceivable circumstances. It must be inflation-proof and impervious to all economic and political events, and its holder must be able to sell it at exactly its inflation-proofed value under all circumstances.

Assume such an instrument can be found, or at least one that approximates to it. Furthermore, take its real yield to be 2 per cent, while on the basis of section 4.2 take the real return on all UK equities to be 8 per cent. Comparing the two returns suggests that equity investors in the market as a whole require a 6 per cent premium to compensate them for the riskiness of their investment. Putting this comparison another way, the yield on all equities equals the risk-free rate of interest plus a risk premium of 6 per cent.

A particular equity may have a return that consistently, or systematically, varies twice as much as the general market return. Such an equity will be twice as risky as an investment in the portfolio of all equities, so that its risk premium will be double that on all equities combined. It is said to have a Beta of 2, which is then applied to the standard risk premium, which is assumed to be 6 per cent, to obtain the return required on the equity. Setting this out in the form of an equation gives:

$$\text{COE} = \text{Risk Free Interest} + \text{Standard Risk Premium} \times \text{Beta} \quad .. \quad (4.2)$$

In this case Beta is 2.0, since the equity's return is twice as variable as the market return, and the share's risk premium is 12 per cent. As the risk-free interest rate is taken to be 2 per cent, investors will only be interested in the equity if it yields at least 14 per cent in real terms.

On the other hand, equities which exhibit less systematic variability than the market will tempt investors to buy them at a yield less than the market average. For example, a share may have a systematic variability of half the market variability. Therefore it will have a Beta of only 0.50, and a risk premium of 3 per cent, and shareholders will expect such an equity to provide a real yield of 5 per cent.

The relation postulated by the CAPM model is appealing: the greater the risk, the greater the expected premium needed to compensate for the increased likelihood of loss. As a first approximation, at least, it is not unreasonable to assume that the premium is proportional to the risk. Consequently the earnings of companies in more risky activities, as represented by the volatility of their equity yields, should be discounted by a correspondingly higher COE.

In explaining the conclusions of the CAPM, we ignored risk as conventionally thought of, but clearly it must be taken on board. An example from banking may help. Major UK banks have very low PE ratios, ranging from under 5 to 1 to around 7 to 1, compared to around 12:1 for the average of other sectors (at August 1988). Many UK banks have loans to problem countries exceeding their net worths, and the longer-term earnings from these assets is problematical. It is likely that the market recognises this and downgrades future earnings from this source accordingly. In fact, the market has replaced current earnings from these assets by its expectation, however rough and ready, of their future earnings. This in part explains the low PE ratios. Projected cashflows, or profits, should always reflect the best estimates of their expected values available, rather than be automatically based on current and past experience. The appropriate COE should then be used to discount these expected values.

4.3.2 The Capital Asset Pricing Model in Practice

As soon as an attempt is made to apply the CAPM, very real problems begin to intrude. First, to calculate the risk premium, the average return achieved by all equities must be estimated. Secondly, a measure of the risk-free rate is needed. Strictly the latter is impossible, so surrogates have to be employed, and usually government bonds or treasury bills are chosen. Both share the stability of being government-guaranteed and so virtually free of credit risk, though this is to confuse a virtual absence of credit risk with an absence of any variation in the real return achieved, a point discussed later. Some practitioners opt for government bonds, since their longer maturities match the longer periods for which equities are usually held. Others prefer treasury bills, believing their short-term nature virtually eliminates any deviation from their expected real return. Unfortunately this view is false, since it is necessary to invest in a series of treasury bills to match the period for which equities are held, and the real return on treasury bills over a significant time period is just as uncertain as that on gilts.

In the UK various measures of the risk premium have been attempted. At the beginning of 1988 Gavyn Davies and Sushill Wadhwani produced an estimate of 6 per cent for the period 1920 to 1987, by taking the difference between the real returns on equities and gilts of 7.5 per cent and 1.5 per cent respectively. For the period 1920 to 1986 Barclays de Zoete Wedd estimated real yields on equities and gilts of 7.7 per cent and 1.5 per cent respectively. In recent years the differential yield has increased. Between 1976 and 1986 the BZW study gives respective real yields on equities and gilts as 15.5 per cent and 6 per cent. Yet not much can be drawn from this comparison, given the artificially high measured return on equities.

Whatever credence is given to the measured risk premium, its derivation is fairly easy. A more sophisticated technique, called regression analysis, is deployed to estimate Betas. The London Business School, for example, calculates them for all quoted UK companies, and updates its estimates each quarter, using the latest sixty sets of monthly yields. One set is the yield on all equities month by month; the other is monthly yields on all individual equities. Yields are defined by formula 4.1, except that the period covered is a month.

The variability of a company's equity yield is then compared to that of all equities. Figure 4.1 gives an indication of the procedure followed. Point A on Figure 4.1 indicates an end month where the yield on all equities over the month was 10 per cent, while Company A's shares yielded 7.5 per cent. The other crosses show relative yields for other months. The line C–D provides the best fit of all the observations. It has a slope of 0.5, indicating that, on average, a 10 per cent change in the yield on all equities is associated with a 5 per cent change in Company A's equity yield.

Beta estimates are widely available in the UK, USA and other countries. Non-quoted companies can base their Betas on those of quoted companies most closely matching their own characteristics. Many companies consist of a number of disparate activities, all of which will have different risk characteristics, and hence Betas. In Chapter 3.4 it was shown that a company should invest in a project, even if its return was far lower than that on existing projects, if it earned its COE. Exactly the same principle applies to a company whose activities have different degrees of risk and correspondingly different Betas; each type of activity, or project, should be assessed against its appropriate COE. All projects with a positive NPV should be undertaken if shareholder value is to be maximised.

FIGURE 4.1 Estimation of Beta

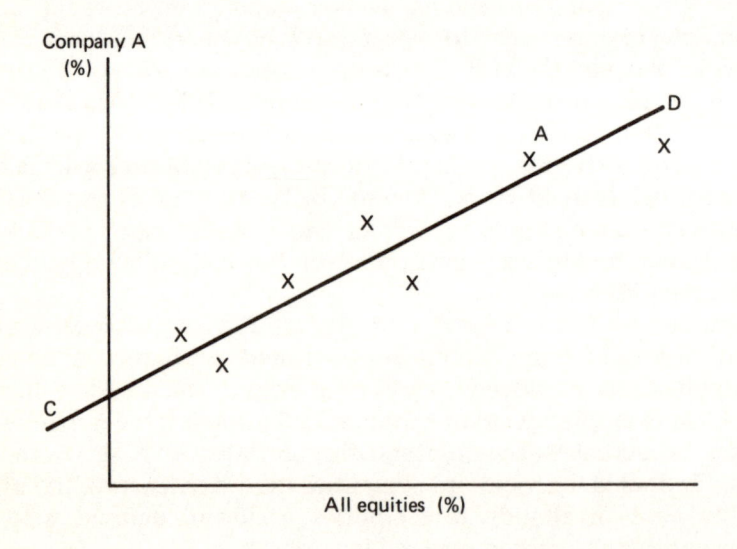

Cost of Equity and the Capital Asset Pricing Model

4.3.3 Critique of the Capital Asset Pricing Model

On the basis of historic performance and shareholder behaviour, it is reasonable to suppose that UK shareholders seek an average real return in the region of 8 per cent. With 10-year gilts yielding 10.25 per cent (August 1988) the CAPM suggests an average COE in the region of 16.25 per cent (that is 6 per cent + 10.25 per cent).

As it stands, the CAPM estimate is of little use; it is a nominal return, and can only be used in evaluation exercises if the profit projections build in an inflation rate consistent with the gilt rate. The current rate of inflation cannot be used as a proxy for the future. An average of estimates by respected forecasters would be better, but would not necessarily be consistent with the market's view. By this approach, the longer-term inflation rate for the UK would be around 4.5 per cent, which gives a real COE of [1.1625/1.045 − 1] × 100, equal to 11.2 per cent. Compared with the long-run rate of 8 per cent, this is very high indeed.

Long-run index-linked UK government bonds give a real yield of around 3.8 per cent. The 6.2 per cent differential between this and the gilt yield might be taken as the market's view of long-run inflation. However, gilts are more risky, since they provide no protection against inflation, and will therefore contain more of a risk premium than index-linked bonds. Consequently the 6.2 per cent will over-estimate the market's view of inflation.

Moreover, problems of inflation apart, today's gilt rate is not a proxy for future interest rates; it is therefore inappropriate to use it for estimating the COE which will then be used to discount cashflows projected many years ahead. A trend real gilt rate would be more appropriate. Taking the long-run average of 1.5 per cent real may not be appropriate. The real return on gilts has increased significantly in recent years and may be as high as 4 per cent. If so, the CAPM gives a real overall COE of 10 per cent, which is still well above long-term historical experience.

Is it plausible, as the CAPM requires, for the COE to increase as interest rates increase? The gilt rate is only a surrogate for the risk-free interest rate, and clearly a poor one at that. Even ignoring the future market values of gilts, not even their future interest rates are known in real terms. Once variations in market value are allowed for, it is a travesty to use gilts as such a proxy. Indeed when stock markets are booming, it is likely that real gilt yields are forced up to match the better returns provided by equities, so that putative cause and effect are reversed. For what it is worth, the BZW data can be used to estimate the Beta of gilts; both prewar and for various postwar periods it does not differ significantly from 0.33. Moreover, the specific risk of interest rate instruments cannot be diversified away. The returns on such instruments of a given tenor and currency are fairly highly correlated. Therefore gilt yields do not provide a firm foundation for estimating the return shareholders seek to earn on equities in general.

Betas are estimated from monthly movements in yields, but this does not reflect shareholder behaviour. Shareholders tend to take the long view, and, from their perspective, movements in share prices are less dominant and dividends more dominant in yield calculations. On this basis the variability in yields will be much less than the CAPM practitioner's estimate. Unfortunately enough data do not exist to provide reliable estimates of Betas that reflect actual shareholder behaviour.

To some extent the character of stock markets may be changing. More funds are now being invested in composite share indices rather than fund managers trying to pick individual winners: in other words, a move to so called passive as opposed to active management. This will tend to reduce the systematic variability of individual shares. Hedging techniques such as futures and options can be used to reduce the risks of capital losses on both equities and interest-bearing instruments. Such techniques will have more impact on equities simply because their price is more variable, and risk premiums should fall as a consequence.

UK government index-linked bonds might, on the face of it, provide a measure of the risk-free rate of interest. Yet even in the space of a year their inflation-proof yields vary too much to be used in this way, as Table 4.4 shows. Nevertheless they clearly set an upper limit. The figures for 5-year bonds suggest a risk-free rate of under 2 per cent, and perhaps 3 per cent for longer term bonds. A compromise rate of 2.5 per cent might be reasonable, and, given the characteristics a true risk-free interest rate must have, this is certainly not low.

With the average real COE set at 8 per cent and the risk-free rate set at 2.5 per cent, the risk premium becomes 5.5 per cent. This premium,

TABLE 4.4 Government Bonds Index-linked Yields

Average gross redemption yields		Fri. Dec. 16	Thur. Dec. 15	Year ago (approx.)	1988 High		1988 Low	
Inflation rate 5%	5yrs	3.75	3.70	3.10	3.75	16/12	2.09	30/3
Inflation rate 5% Over 5yrs		3.77	3.77	3.96	4.27	13/1	3.53	8/11
Inflation rate 10%	5yrs	2.46	2.58	3.49	3.59	13/1	1.09	30/3
Inflation rate 10% Over 5yrs		3.59	3.61	4.03	4.37	13/1	3.37	8/11

Source: *Financial Times*, 16 December 1988.

combined with the assumed risk-free rate and Betas estimated in the usual way, can be used to calculate the COE for individual companies, though the caveats made on the way Betas are estimated must not be forgotten.

Most of the criticisms of the CAPM model have not attacked the theory but its practical applications. Normally these require assumptions that on examination are simply untenable. Ways can be found to circumvent some of these problems, but even then they require using conventional estimates of Beta, which may be too high. Nevertheless they are the best we have, and their judicious use is better than ignoring the problem of relative risk.

4.4 Conclusions

Estimating the COE is difficult, and probably more judgemental than scientific. Use of the CAPM in the UK gives rise to a future COE that is outside long-run historical experience, and also contrary to observed shareholder behaviour and somewhat optimistic assumptions about future productivity. Ultimately it is for individual managers, finance directors or executive committees to take their own views. However, they are warned not to be blinded by spurious science, though it would be wrong to make judgements without an understanding of the theories employed, their shortcomings and historical experience.

5

TRADITIONAL CASHFLOW ANALYSIS

5.1 Why Cashflows?

Investors, whether individual or corporate, are interested in what they pay out, what they receive and the anticipated timing of these flows. Anything else is at best an irrelevancy, or at worst obscures what is really happening. In Chapter 2 it was shown that conventional accounting measures are arbitrary, as they often bear little relation to the reality they supposedly represent.

The real concern of a company that invests in a factory is whether or not it will generate sufficient cash to cover the company's COE. Accounting profits, owing to the arbitrary nature of depreciation charges and other accounting conventions, do not help in this assessment. For example, accountants debit tax against profits in the year the latter occur, though corporation tax is not paid until at least a year after the financial year to which it relates. The fact that payment is delayed by at least a year is a clear gain; the tax payment will be discounted more heavily, reflecting the fact that the taxpayer is in effect making the company a loan on which it can earn its COE.

Audited accounts will sometimes contain provisions for costs that will have to be met at a later date. For example, provisions might be made against this year's profits to meet known exceptional costs, such as redundancies, which will occur in subsequent years. However, such provisions do not reflect actual payments or cash outflows, so they should only be included when actual payment can reasonably be anticipated, or the project will appear less profitable that it is simply because some costs have not been discounted heavily enough.

Table 5.1 illustrates the impact of ignoring the delayed tax payment. In this example an initial investment outlay of £10m generates pre-tax profits, assumed to equal cashflow, of £4.5m for 5 years. After tax at 40 per cent is charged, profits after tax become £2.7m. If this post-tax profit stream is discounted at 14 per cent and the initial investment deducted, the NPV is minus £0.73m. On this basis the scheme is not worthwhile.

Traditional Cashflow Analysis

TABLE 5.1 Impact of Delayed Tax Payment: Discounting at 14 per cent (£m)

End of year	Investment outlay	Pre-tax profit	Tax	PAT	Discounted PAT	Cashflow	Discounted cashflow
0	10.00			(10.00)	(10.00)	(10.00)	(10.00)
1		4.50	1.8	2.70	2.37	4.50	3.95
2		4.50	1.8	2.70	2.08	2.70	2.08
3		4.50	1.8	2.70	1.82	2.70	1.82
4		4.50	1.8	2.70	1.60	2.70	1.60
5		4.50	1.8	2.70	1.40	2.70	1.40
6						(1.80)	(0.82)
NPV					(0.73)		0.03

If, however, tax due is not paid until the end of the following year, the position is as shown under the 'Cashflow' column. In year 1 no tax is paid, even though it is due, so that the cashflow is £4.5m. In year 2 the previous year's tax is paid. The post-tax profit and the cashflow, in this example, are now the same. The tax paid in year 5 is that due on year 4's profit. Year 5's tax is paid in year 6. When the cashflows are discounted at 14 per cent, the NPV is positive, showing that the project is worthwhile.

Another important difference between accounting profits and DCF analysis is their treatment of stocks. In accounting terms the profit and loss account is drawn up in Table 5.2.

This statement represents the first year profit and loss account for a new business. During the year £2m was spent on materials, but at the end of the year a quarter of them had not been processed and sold. Accountants would argue that these unsold items, though bought this

TABLE 5.2 Accounting Profits and Stocks (£m)

	Costs		Revenues
Purchases	2.0	Sales	2.0
Plus opening stocks	0.0		
Less closing stocks	0.5		
	1.5		
Profit/(Loss)	0.5		
	2.0		2.0

year, should really be a cost against the following year's profit. For this reason closing stocks and/or raw materials are deducted from total purchases during the year. Had there been any opening stocks, these would have been added to purchases. Thus in this first year of operation a profit of £0.5m is registered, though in cashflow terms there is no gain or loss. Outgoings amounted to £2m, not £1.5m, and revenues only amounted to £2m. Clearly, the cashflow view is the real measure of what is happening, while the accountant's convention hides the reality of the situation.

In the second year, and assuming no growth, opening and closing stocks would be equal. Therefore they cancel out and the P & L and cashflow statements give the same picture. However, if only the P & L figures had been taken, the first year's investment of £0.5m in stocks would have been ignored. Moreover, if the company grows, closing stocks will usually exceed opening stocks, and only a cashflow approach will pick up actual cash payments.

Debtors and creditors are similar to stocks in their impact on the P & L account. Sales made this year but not yet paid for are represented by debtors. Year end, or closing, debtors are added to actual revenues received, and opening debtors deducted. The rationale for the accountant's approach is understandable. After all, sales made this year, even if not paid for, do belong to it; nevertheless money owed is not available to the firm either to reinvest or offset payments, and must be excluded from cashflow statements.

Creditors are the exact opposite of debtors: they represent items purchased but not paid for. In the P & L closing creditors are added to costs and opening creditors deducted. However, until payment is actually made, there is no drain on the firm's cash resources. The net impact on the P & L of stocks, debtors and creditors is called working capital; for most companies this is positive and in a cashflow context will usually lead to a deduction from accounting profits as companies and their working capital grow.

The more important and common differences between accounting profits and cashflow statements have been noted. They are not exhaustive, but the correct principle has been demonstrated. Only items that are cash inflows or outflows, during a specific period, should be included in that period's cashflow statement.

5.2 Cashflow and Shareholder Value

Cash, not accounting profits, determines the worth of any investment. This principle can be extended to consider a company as a whole or one of

Traditional Cashflow Analysis

its major business divisions, so that, from the outside, the concept of the return on an individual investment or project can lose its clarity of definition. A business consists of a whole series of projects, some undertaken simultaneously, others following on. Nevertheless it is easy, in principle, to consider the future net cashflows of an enterprise, and hence its present value. Its future stream of profits can be estimated, and the necessary adjustments made to convert these to cashflows. Investments in fixed assets can be estimated, perhaps on the basis of known expansion plans, likely market growth and developments, and past experience. Of course the company itself should be able to make a far better job of this than the shareholders.

Such estimated cashflows will reflect all payments the company needs to make, including expenditure on plant, equipment and new facilities generally. These cashflows therefore will show the maximum dividends that can be paid, and discounting them at the company's COE will give an estimate of the company's present value. If the market capitalisation of its shares is higher, they are a bad buy, and vice versa. Negative cashflows indicate that the company will only be able to maintain its expected growth if it can raise new funds. Additional funds will have to be raised to allow dividend payments. This is not necessarily harmful, provided subsequent cashflows are high enough to offset the negative flows.

5.3 Profits, Balance Sheets and Cashflows

The reasons for cashflow analysis, rather than the use of accounting profits, have been shown. This section shows the relation between accounting figures and cashflows, using published accounts. UK companies are required to produce a 'statement of sources and application of funds', which in fact is a cashflow statement, and ICI's 1987 accounts are used to illustrate the relations between profits, the balance sheet and cashflows in Table 5.3, 5.4 and 5.5.

The profit and loss account (Table 5.3) shows a 'net profit for the financial year' of £760m and retained profit of £483m. Yet the statement of sources and applications of funds (S&AF, Table 5.5) shows a cash deficit of £247m – a difference of £1.034bn. The explanations for this huge difference are straightforward.

The S&AF starts with trading profit taken from the profit and loss account and the following adjustments are made:

FINANCIAL DECISION-MAKING

TABLE 5.3   ICI Profit and Loss Account for the Year Ended
31 December 1987

	1987 £m	1986 £m
TURNOVER	11,123	10,136
Operating costs	(10,001)	(9,232)
Other operating income	175	145
TRADING PROFIT	1,297	1,049
Share of profits less losses of related companies	157	95
Net interest payable	(142)	(128)
PROFIT ON ORDINARY ACTIVITIES BEFORE TAXATION	1,312	1,016
Tax on profit on ordinary activities	(504)	(382)
PROFIT ON ORDINARY ACTIVITIES AFTER TAXATION	808	634
Attributable to minorities	(48)	(34)
NET PROFIT ATTRIBUTABLE TO PARENT COMPANY	760	600
Extraordinary item	–	(43)
NET PROFIT FOR THE FINANCIAL YEAR	760	557
Dividends	(227)	(238)
PROFIT RETAINED FOR YEAR	483	319

- Depreciation charges are book entries and do not reflect actual cash payments, so they are added to profits.
- Profits include £19m of government grants owed to ICI but not yet paid, so the amount must be deducted.
- Dividends received from related companies must be added to trading profits.
- Various miscellaneous items have been credited to profits, but at year end £9m remained unpaid.
- Interest paid is an obvious deduction.
- The tax deduction of £349m actually paid is considerably less than the £504m shown in the accounts.
- Dividends of £283m were paid during the year, and are deducted from profits.
- However, cashflow analysis normally considers the situation before dividends are paid, as the objective is to estimate the dividends that could be paid. On this basis they would not be deducted, and the £274m deficit shown in the S&AF statement would become a positive cashflow of £9m.

Traditional Cashflow Analysis

TABLE 5.4   ICI Balance Sheet as at 31 December 1987

	Group 1987 £m	1986 £m
ASSETS EMPLOYED		
FIXED ASSETS		
Tangible assets	3,750	3,912
Investments: Subsidiaries		
Related and other companies	417	333
	4,167	4,245
CURRENT ASSETS		
Stocks	1,812	1,734
Debtors	2,162	2,015
Investments and short-term deposits	494	471
Cash	152	221
	4,620	4,441
TOTAL ASSETS	8,787	8,686
CREDITORS DUE WITHIN A YEAR		
Short-term borrowings	(559)	(441)
Current instalments of loans	(46)	(74)
Other creditors	(2,365)	(2,022)
	(2,970)	(2,537)
NET CURRENT ASSETS (LIABILITIES)	1,650	1,904
TOTAL ASSETS LESS CURRENCY LIABILITIES	5,817	6,149
FINANCED BY		
CREDITORS DUE AFTER A YEAR		
Loans	1,511	1,538
Other creditors	70	83
	1,581	1,621
PROVISIONS	295	276
GRANTS NOT YET CREDITED TO PROFIT	139	183
MINORITY INTERESTS	357	404
CAPITAL AND RESERVES	3,445	3,665
	5,817	6,149

- Expenditure on fixed assets and acquisitions, net of any sales, amounted to £1112m, and is deducted.
- Stocks increased £169m and debtors £68m; they have to be deducted for the reasons noted in the previous two sections.

TABLE 5.5 ICI Statement of Sources and Applications of Funds

	1987 £m	1986 £m
SOURCES		
FUNDS GENERATED FROM OPERATIONS		
Trading profit	1,297	1,049
Depreciation	464	491
Petroleum revenue tax paid, less provided		(42)
Government grants credited to profit, less received	(19)	(9)
Dividends from related companies	65	56
Miscellaneous items, including exchange	(9)	(60)
	1,798	1,485
LESS: INTEREST AND TAXATION PAID DURING THE YEAR		
Interest (net)	(141)	(125)
Taxation	(349)	(298)
SOURCES NET OF INTEREST AND TAXATION	1,308	1,062
APPLICATIONS		
DIVIDENDS PAID DURING YEAR	283	249
FIXED ASSETS		
Tangible assets	708	643
Disposals of tangible assets	(26)	(35)
Acquisitions and new investments	544	578
Disposals of subsidiaries and related company investments	(114)	(30)
	1,112	1,156
WORKING CAPITAL CHANGES		
Stocks increase (1986 decrease)	169	(115)
Debtors increase (1986 decrease)	68	(45)
Creditors and provisions increase (excl. dividends and taxation) (1986 decrease)	(50)	66
	187	(94)
TOTAL APPLICATIONS	1,582	1,311
DEFICIT	(274)	(249)
FINANCED BY		
Issues of ICI Ordinary Stock	140	50
Repayment of ICI Preference Stock		(7)
Other external finance	(6)	(7)
Net repayment of loans (1986 net new borrowings)	(24)	178
Increase in short-term borrowings (1986 decrease)	118	(70)
Decrease in cash and short-term investments	46	105
	274	249

Traditional Cashflow Analysis

- Similarly the £50m increase in creditors can be added.

In summary, the position is as shown in Table 5.6.

TABLE 5.6 Comparisons of ICI's Profits and Cashflows (£m)

	1987	1986
Cashflow	(274)	(249)
Add dividends	283	249
Gives cashflow	9	–
Profits	760	557

Thus the distinction between profit and cashflow is very far from nominal. The differences are primarily explained by the difference between expenditure on assets, on the one hand, and depreciation plus changes in working capital, on the other. Whether or not ICI's current negligible cashflows are a good or bad thing depends entirely upon the future cashflows they generate. The view taken on this must ultimately depend upon how capable the management is judged to be.

5.4 Bygones are Bygones

A multi-billion pound project is in trouble. Originally its capital expenditure was forecast at £5bn, and its completion time at 5 years. Latest estimates suggest completion will take 7 years and total costs will amount to £6.5bn. On the basis of these figures the project will only earn 10 per cent, against a COE of 12.5 per cent. The question is therefore whether to abandon the project and cut investors' losses or carry on.

Although the project will now fail to earn its COE, this is irrelevant to the decision, and the money spent to date, even if it is £3bn, is of no consequence. Cashflow analysis is only concerned with future costs and revenues. Latest projections may indicate future expenditure of £3.5bn over the next 4 years, while revised running cost and revenue forecasts suggest the return on the remaining £3.5bn of capital expenditure will be 14 per cent. This latest estimate exceeds the project's COE, and the project should continue.

The £3bn already spent is lost, and nothing can be done about it, however unwise in retrospect the decision for commitment. Bankers that have lent funds will still have to pay interest on their own deposits and borrowings, whatever happens to the scheme. Shareholders have committed their cash, and if the project is abandoned, they will never see any of their money again. On the other hand, if the scheme goes ahead, shareholders will earn 14 per cent on the additional funds they commit, i.e. 1.5 percentage points more than alternative equivalent risk outlets. Clearly it is in their interest for the scheme to continue. This will also be true for the scheme's bankers.

Nevertheless the banks may choose to put the project into liquidation. The banks, depending upon their loan agreements, may have no obligations to the project's shareholders now that it has failed to live up to expectations. The project is now expected to return 14 per cent on the remaining capital expenditure, against a 12.5 per cent COE. Hence it will have a positive NPV. If this is, say, £400m, a new group of shareholders may be prepared to pay the banks £250m to take the project on, allowing the banks to reduce their losses to date by this amount. Alternatively, the banks might come to an arrangement with the existing shareholders. Such an arrangement would give the banks a free equity stake for their continuing support, but would only be worthwhile to them if the PV of their stake was at least £250m.

This example is an illustration of the principle that past expenditures are irrelevant, that bygones are bygones and that only future cashflows should affect decision-making.

5.5 Weighted Cost of Capital

5.5.1 Equity Flows

Traditional cashflow analysis always takes into the cash outflows 100 per cent of the project's capital expenditure. Yet in practice projects are financed both by equity and various forms of debt. Since contemporary corporate finance theory is concerned with maximising shareholder value, it might appear more natural to look at equity cashflows. Thus a project might be financed 60 per cent by equity and 40 per cent by debt. Assuming, for simplicity, that the latter is entirely by way of overdraft, the equity flows could be those shown in Table 5.7.

A project costing £100m yields £27.06m each year for 5 years, before payment of interest. Interest is charged at 5 per cent on the £40m financed by overdraft, so that the cashflow after interest (the equity flow) is £25.06m a year. Against these flows must be set the initial equity invest-

Traditional Cashflow Analysis

TABLE 5.7   Equity Cashflows (£m)

End of year	Capital expenditure	Cashflow before interest	Interest at 5%	Cashflow after interest	NPV at 15%
0	100.00	(100.00)	2.00	(60.00)	(60.00)
1		27.06	2.00	25.06	21.79
2		27.06	2.00	25.06	18.95
3		27.06	2.00	25.06	16.48
4		27.06	2.00	25.06	14.33
5		27.06	2.00	(14.94)	(7.43)
NPV					4.11

ment of £60m and repayment of the overdraft at the end of year 5. With these assumptions, the NPV is £4.11m. All this is fine – but impossible. There is no money to repay the overdraft at the end of year 5. All the equity flows have been paid out as dividends. Rather than leaving the overdraft payment to year 5, it could have been paid off over the 5 years. This delays payment to the shareholders, and they lose out because of the impact discounting has on delayed dividends.

5.5.2   Weighted Cost of Capital

Initially it was assumed that the project was 60 per cent equity- and 40 per cent debt-financed. If the 60:40 ratio was the best ratio to start with, then it is likely to remain the best throughout the project's life. Moreover the market will have a view on what equity to debt ratios are appropriate for various types of activities. Lower equity to debt ratios will make a business more risky, since it will have a greater burden of fixed costs to meet out of variable profits. Thus, as the equity to debt ratio falls and the riskiness increases, the COE will tend to increase.

Taking the weighted cost of equity and debt gives a weighted cost of capital of:

$$11\% = 0.6 \times 15\% + 0.4 \times 5\%$$

This can be used to discount the pre-interest cashflows of Table 5.8.

In this table no interest has been deducted from the cashflows, and total capital expenditure is deducted. These cashflows are discounted at 11 per cent, and the NPV is zero. This compares to the positive NPV of £4.11m in Table 5.7.

FINANCIAL DECISION-MAKING

TABLE 5.8   Weighted Cost of Capital at 11 per cent

End of year	Cashflow	Discounted cashflow
0	(100.00)	(100.00)
1	27.06	24.38
2	27.06	21.96
3	27.06	19.78
4	27.06	17.82
5	27.06	16.06
		0.00

To summarise, the weighted cost of capital approach incorporates borrowing costs into the average cost of capital. When this method is used therefore, interest payments should be excluded from the cashflows, otherwise double counting occurs, while all of the capital expenditure is treated as a negative cashflow.

5.5.3 The Capital Asset Pricing Model Again

In section 5.5.2 it was suggested that the COE would probably increase as the proportion of capital funds represented by debt increased. In spite of the attractions of this argument, a project manager may decide that, while he cannot do much about his cashflows, he can manipulate his cost of capital. Initially his costs of debt and equity may be 8 per cent and 14 per cent, with weights of 25 per cent and 75 per cent respectively, giving an overall capital cost of:

$$0.25 \times 8\% + 0.75 \times 14\% = 12.5\%$$

With this cost of capital the project may have problems breaking even. Consequently the project manager decides to increase the debt ratio to 50 per cent to get a lower capital cost, amounting to:

$$0.05 \times 8\% + 0.05 \times 14\% = 11\%$$

As already noted, this approach will not work. As the company's debt increases, it becomes more highly geared or leveraged, producing a weaker balance sheet and adding to the risk. With increased risk, shareholders will expect a higher return, and the COE will now exceed 14 per

Traditional Cashflow Analysis

cent. The CAPM can be used to provide a more rigorous demonstration of this contention.

The market value of a company's assets must equal the market value of the liabilities funding the assets. Initially assume that the assets are fully funded by equity, in which case the Beta of the assets will equal the equity's Beta. More probably the assets will be funded by debt and equity, so that the asset's Beta will be an appropriately weighted average of the debt and equity Betas. However, the variability of profit before interest will be invariant to the debt equity mix. In other words, the assets' Beta will be constant. From this reasoning the following weighted average relationship can be stated:

$$\text{Beta}(A) = \text{Beta}(E)[E/(D+E)] + \text{Beta}(D)[D/(D+E)]$$

where A are the assets, E the equity and D the debt.

This equation can be rearranged to state:

$$\text{Beta}(E) = \text{Beta}(A) \frac{(D+E)}{E} - \text{Beta}(D) \frac{D}{E}$$

That is:

$$\text{Beta}(E) = \text{Beta}(A) + [\text{Beta}(A) - \text{Beta}(D)] \frac{D}{E} \quad \quad (5.1)$$

By definition the weighted cost of capital (WCC) equals:

$$[E/(D+E)]\text{COE} + [D/(D+E)][\text{Debt Interest}] \quad \quad (5.2)$$

By means of the CAPM and equation 5.1 for the Beta of equity it can be shown that the WCC is constant. Remember:

$$\text{COE} = I(F) + P\text{Beta}(E) \quad \quad (5.3)$$

where $I(F)$ = risk-free rate of interest
P = risk premium

On substituting Beta (E) from equation 5.1 into equation 5.3 the COE becomes:

$$\text{COE} = I(F) + P[\text{Beta}(A) + (\text{Beta}(A) - \text{Beta}(D)) \frac{D}{E}] \quad \quad (5.4)$$

[49]

FINANCIAL DECISION-MAKING

Again using the CAPM, interest on debt can be written:

$$I(D) = I(F) + P\,Beta(D) \hspace{2cm} (5.5)$$

where $I(D)$ = interest on debt

On substituting 5.4 and 5.5 into equation 5.2 the WCC becomes:

$$WCC = I(F) + PBeta(A)$$

Of the terms on the RHS, the risk-free interest rate and the risk premium are constant, given the assumptions of the CAPM. It has been further assumed that the assets' Beta is constant, since pre-interest profits do not vary with the capital structure. From this it follows that the WCC is constant, and therefore independent of the debt to equity ratio.

All this is a bit arid, so it is time to breathe some life into things by way of an example. Initially assume that an asset is funded entirely by equity, and for simplicity's assume that its Beta is 1.0, and hence the equity's Beta is 1.0. Further assume that the return on equities in general is 15 per cent and is consistent with the relationship 15% = 9% + 6% × 1. The balance sheet and profit and loss account will be:

		£m	
Asset	100	Profit before interest	15
		Interest	—
Equity	100	Profit after interest	15
Debt	—		
	100	ROE	15%

and a £1m increase in profits will increase the ROE to 16 per cent.

Now assume that the same asset is funded 50/50 equity and debt. The balance sheet and profit and loss account become:

		£m	
Asset	100	Profit before interest	15
		Interest (at 12%)	6
Equity	50	Profit after interest	9
Debt	50		
	100	ROE	18%

Traditional Cashflow Analysis

According to the CAPM the equity's Beta should now be 1.5, that is (18–9)/6. Likewise the debt's Beta should be 0.5, that is (12–9)/6.

What happens if profit before interest increases by £1m? The return on the asset has increased 1 per cent, and it has a Beta of 1.0. According to the CAPM, the debt has a Beta of 0.5, so that its return should increase 0.5 per cent to 12.5 per cent. If it does, the profit and loss account becomes:

	£m
Profit before interest	16.00
Interest (at 12.5%)	6.25
Profit after interest	9.75
ROE	19.50%

The ROE has increased by 1.5 per cent to 19.5 per cent. Thus in this second case the ROE is 50 per cent more variable than in the first, while its Beta is 50 per cent higher. Finally note that the WCC is 18% × 0.5 + 12% × 0.5 = 15%. Thus all the required relationships hold.

5.5.4 Repayment Assumptions

Accepting that rough and ready assumptions have to be made, then discounting cashflows at the weighted cost of capital appears sensible. Nevertheless, there is yet another set of implicit assumptions. The approach assumes a specific repayment pattern of both borrowings and equity from the project's cashflows. Both shareholders and lenders must have their principal repaid exactly in proportion to the project's economic depreciation charges; any other pattern of repayment will be inconsistent with the assumed returns to shareholders and lenders, as Table 5.9 shows.

The second column shows the asset's true economic worth, taken to equal book value, at the end of each year. These values are derived from the cashflows, or profits before depreciation, shown in the next column. The IRR of these pre-depreciation profits, in relation to the asset's cost, is 16 per cent. The annual depreciation charges reflect the declining value of the asset, and are the economic depreciation charges derived in section 2.9. Since the asset's book value reflects its true economic worth, year-end profits after depreciation will always equal 16 per cent of the asset's opening value.

It is assumed that the project is funded 60 per cent equity and 40 per

FINANCIAL DECISION-MAKING

TABLE 5.9   Repayment Assumptions (£m)

End of year	Asset's book value	Profit before dep.	Dep.	Profit after dep.	Profit on BV	Equity cashflow	Lenders' cashflow
1	100						
2	80	36.0	20.0	16.0	16%	21.60	14.40
3	55	37.8	25.0	12.8	16%	22.68	15.12
4	25	38.8	30.0	8.8	16%	23.28	15.52
5	0	29.0	25.0	4.0	16%	17.40	11.60
PV		100.0				60.0	40.0

cent debt, with respective costs of 20 per cent and 10 per cent. The weighted cost of capital is thus 16 per cent, and if the cashflows in column 2 are discounted at this rate, their PV is £100m and the project just breaks even. Allocation of 60 per cent of pre-depreciation profits to shareholders gives the cashflows in the penultimate column. When discounted at 20 per cent, their present value is £60m, and shareholders just break even. The remaining profits before depreciation are allocated to lenders; discounting them at 10 per cent generates a £40m present value and lenders also just break even.

The monies received by lenders and shareholders consist of interest payments and repayments of principal. Thus lenders receive 40 per cent of the cashflow each year. In effect, this consists of 40 per cent of the depreciation charge, representing principal, and 40 per cent of the profit after depreciation, representing interest. This means lenders have to have their principal repaid in exact proportion to the economic depreciation charges; any other repayment pattern of principal and interest would not give them a return of 10 per cent. It could be higher or lower. Exactly the same applies to shareholders. However, once the appropriate pattern of equity flows is known, it would then be possible to discount them at their appropriate COE.

In the following chapters new ideas are introduced. To ease exposition the COE will be treated as invariant to banks' capital structures. This question will be revisited in Chapter 14.

PART TWO

6

BANK REGULATION AND CAPITAL ADEQUACY

6.1 Introduction

Banking systems are so important to the efficient and safe functioning of economies that they have usually been subject to some form of supervision. To date such supervision has been national in character, but in recent years it has started to take on an international dimension. The initiative came from the Bank of England and the USA Federal Reserve. In January 1987 these two supervisory bodies published a paper, 'Convergence of Capital Adequacy in the UK and US', which formed the background to the Committee on Banking Regulations and Supervisory Practices report of July 1988, more commonly known as the BIS report.

The BIS report committed the 'Group of Ten' major industrial countries to introduce more or less common standards of capital adequacy by the end of 1992. Two basic objectives are intended to be served by the report's recommendations. First, the new framework should strengthen the balance sheets of many banks and so generate greater confidence in the international banking system. Second, since lowly capitalised, or highly geared, banks it is held can charge their customers less while achieving an adequate return on equity, a further objective is to create a fairer competitive environment by reducing such differentials.

6.2 Risk-weighted Assets

Different assets are subject to various degrees of credit risk. There can be no default with respect to cash held by a bank, and it has a zero risk weighting, but at the other extreme unsecured lending is considered to be subject to the maximum risk of default and is given a weighting of 1.0. Lending fully secured by a mortgage on residential property is judged to be of intermediate risk and has a 0.50 weighting, while claims on OECD banks are considered less risky still and carry a risk weighting of 0.2. Annex 1 to this chapter (p. 62) gives a complete list of the BIS risk weightings.

Risk in this context is quite a different concept than that associated with the CAPM, which defines risk as the variability of returns. Here risk is defined in its more common usage to mean the likelihood of default after realisation of any collateral held. In other words it is the credit risk.

6.2.1 Conventional Contingents

Off balance sheet items, or contingents, are also subject to risk. A guarantee is subject to exactly the same risk of default as the loan being guaranteed, and hence has a 'credit conversion' factor of 1.0. However, if the guarantee is issued by an OECD bank, the credit conversion factor is multiplied by 0.2 to reflect the risk weighting applied to such a bank. On the other hand, if the guarantee was issued by a company, and without appropriate collateral, it would be multiplied by 1.0 to reflect the company's risk weighting. Annex 2 (p. 65) shows the credit conversion factors applied to most types of conventional contingents.

6.2.2 Interest Rate and Foreign Exchange Contingents

In addition to conventional contingents such as guarantees, letters of credit and bonds, there are the newer hedging instruments. These are the interest rate related contingencies, which include instruments such as forward rate agreements and interest rate swaps. Although far from new, forward foreign exchange agreements are included in this group. All have one basic characteristic in common: the future variability of the interest or FX rate hedged gives rise to a credit risk if one party to the transaction cannot meet its obligations.

There are two approaches to estimating the credit conversion factors to be applied to these instruments. The majority of the 'Group of Ten' central banks favour the current exposure method. A bank might suffer a loss if a particular party to a transaction defaulted. Such a loss would be the PV of the future costs to the bank of undertaking the defaulter's obligations, or it would be the cost of going to the market and paying a third party to undertake the commitment. The consequent credit exposure is known as 'marking to market'. Owing to the volatility of interest and FX rates, future potential exposure over the contract's life could be more than current exposure. This potential future credit exposure is

Bank Regulation and Capital Adequacy

related to the remaining length of the contract as well as the volatility of the rate hedged. On the basis of detailed theoretical and empirical studies the factors in Table 6.1 are added to the current level of credit exposure.

An alternative method of estimating credit exposure avoids the two-step approach of the current exposure approach. In this simpler approach, called the original exposure method, the nominal values of contracts are weighted according to maturity and volatility (see Table 6.2).

TABLE 6.1   Current Exposure Method: Future Risk Additions

Residual maturity	Interest rate contracts (%)	Exchange rate contracts (%)
Less than a year	zero	1.0
One year and over	0.5	5.0

TABLE 6.2   Original Exposure Method: Weightings on Principal Amounts

Maturity	Interest rate contracts (%)	Exchange rate contracts (%)
Less than a year	0.5	2.0
One year and less than 2 years	1.0	5.0
For each additional year	1.0	3.0

It is open to the authorities in each country which of these methods they choose.

Once the credit equivalent amounts have been calculated by one of these methods, they are then multiplied by the appropriate counter party weighting, in exactly the same way as it is done for a conventional contingent, except that a 50 per cent weight will apply to counter parties that would otherwise have a 100 per cent weight.

6.2.3   An Example

A simplified balance sheet and list of contingents are shown in Table 6.3, along with the calculation of risk-weighted assets (RWA). The first

FINANCIAL DECISION-MAKING

TABLE 6.3 Calculation of Risk-weighted Assets

	£m	Weight	RWAs
Assets			
Cash	100	0.0	—
Deposits with OECD banks	1000	0.2	200
Mortgages	5000	0.5	2500
Lending to private sector	20,000	1.0	20,000
	26,100		22,700
Conventional contingents			
Sight LCs issued by OECD banks	1000	0.04[1]	40
Sight LCs	1000	0.20	200
Performance bonds issued by private sector	500	0.50	250
Guarantees issued by private sector	500	1.00	500
	3000		990
Interest rate and FX contingents: original exposure method			
Forward rate agreement with private sector (2-year maturities)	2000	0.010	20
180-day FX contracts with OECD banks	20,000	0.004[2]	80
180-day FX contracts with private sector	5000	0.010	50
	27,000		150
Total risk-weighted assets			23,840

NOTES:
1 Credit exposure for sight LCs is 0.2 (Annex 2). OECD banks have a risk weighting of 0.2, so that the overall risk weighting is 0.2 × 0.2 = 0.04.
2 The credit exposure for a 180-day FX contract is 0.02 (Table 6.2). OECD banks have a risk weighting of 0.2, so that the overall risk weighting is 0.02 × 0.20 = 0.004.

column shows the value of assets and contingents. The second column, which shows the weights to be applied, is compiled from Annexes 1 and 2 and Table 6.2.

In the case of balance sheet assets, calculation of the associated RWA is straightforward. Mortgage lending, for example, is given a risk weighting of 0.5 and the £5000m of mortgages outstanding is multiplied by 0.5 to get a risk-weighted equivalent of £2500m.

Contingents are slightly more complicated. First, the credit exposure equivalent must be determined. In the case of a sight LC its credit equivalent weighting is 0.20, so that £1000m of such LCs issued on behalf of a commercial client would have an RWA of £200m. But OECD banks have a risk weighting of 0.2, so that such an LC issued by an OECD bank would have an overall risk weighting of 0.20 × 0.20 = 0.04 when confirmed. Consequently confirmed sight LCs of £1000m issued by OECD banks have a RWA equivalent of only £40m. The rest of the schedule is similarly constructed. In sum the RWAs amount to £23,840m (Table 6.3), and they must be supported by a prudent level of capital, as determined by the BIS regulations.

6.3 Capital Adequacy

6.3.1 Equity: First Tier Capital

BIS breaks out capital into two basic components: core capital or basic equity, which will be called first tier capital; and supplementary capital, which will be called second tier capital.

Equity, i.e. cash injections from shareholders and retained earnings, is considered to be the fundamental constituent of capital. If profits suffer, then legally, if not in practice, no dividends need be paid. Equity is always available to meet losses and contribute to a bank's solvency, whatever vicissitudes the bank may suffer. Perpetual non-cumulative preference shares are treated as equity. Minority interests are also included, since the assets in which the minorities have an interest are given a full risk weighting.

6.3.2 Second Tier Capital

While equity provides the most fundamental underpinning of the balance sheet, other forms of capital also provide support in times of difficulty. They are defined below.

Undisclosed reserves
Many banks maintain undisclosed reserves in order to hide significant variations in profits. Provided they can otherwise be legitimately shown as published retained profits, they can be taken into secondary capital.

Revaluation reserves
For the purposes of capital adequacy these are formal property revaluation surpluses, and the difference between the book value of securities and their market value. In both cases they must be prudently valued to reflect the possibilities of price fluctuations and forced sale. However,

surpluses on equities are subject to a 55 per cent discount to reflect their market volatility and the capital gains tax that would be suffered on their realisation. Interestingly there is no requirement to deduct the potential capital gains tax from property surpluses.

General provisions
These are created against possible future losses, over and above the specific provisions against assets in danger of default. Thus 'general provisions' against LDC countries' debts would not count as secondary capital. By 1992 any general provisions in excess of 1.25 per cent of risk assets will not count towards secondary capital.

Hybrid debt instruments
These are instruments that combine characteristics of equity and debt, and they must meet the following requirements:

- Be *unsecured*, subordinated and *fully paid-up*.
- *Not be redeemable* at the initiative of the holder or without the prior consent of the supervisory authority.
- Be available to participate in losses without the bank being obliged to cease trading (unlike conventional subordinated debt).
- Although the capital instrument may carry an obligation to pay interest that cannot permanently be reduced or waived (unlike dividends on ordinary shareholders' equity), *it should allow service obligations to be deferred* (as with cumulative preference shares) where the profitability of the bank would not support payment.

Examples are perpetual subordinated floating rate notes, mandatory convertible debt instruments and long-term preferred shares.

Subordinated debt
Conventional unsecured subordinated debt capital instruments with a minimum original fixed term to maturity of over 5 years, and limited life redeemable preference shares, can be included in second tier capital. During the last 5 years to maturity an annual discount of 20 per cent of the principal value will be applied each year to reflect the diminishing value of these instruments as a continuing source of strength. Unlike hybrid instruments, these are not normally available to participate in the losses of a bank which continues trading. For this reason these instruments are limited to a maximum of 50 per cent of first tier capital.

Bank Regulation and Capital Adequacy

6.3.3 Deductions from Capital

Goodwill must be deducted from first tier capital. Non-consolidated subsidiaries engaged in banking and financial activities must be deducted from total capital. The Bank of England takes a more stringent line and requires all trade investments and non-consolidated subsidiaries to be deducted from capital. Taking the banking system as a whole, inclusion of other banks' capital in the capital base amounts to double counting. Therefore national supervisory authorities may, at their own discretion, deduct from capital a bank's holdings of capital issued by other banks or deposit-taking institutions. The Bank of England will continue to deduct these holdings from capital.

6.3.4 The Minimum Capital Ratio

The minimum capital ratio in relation to risk-weighted assets has been set at 8 per cent. Of this, first tier capital must be at least 50 per cent; in other words, risk-weighted assets must be supported by at least 4 per cent equity. It is well known that the Bank of England will be setting significantly tougher standards, and will probably require a capital ratio of at least 10 per cent.

Capital adequacy can now be summarised by the following relations:

$$(E-GW) + S - UI - D \geq aRWA, \text{ and}$$
$$(E-GW) \geq 0.5\,[(E - GW) + S - UI - D]$$

where E is the first-tier capital, S the second tier capital, GW the goodwill, UI the unconsolidated investments in financial subsidiaries, D the deductions at national discretion, RWA the total risk-weighted assets, and a the required capital ratio.

These formalised relations simply say that total capital after required deductions must at least equal risk-weighted assets times the required capital ratio, and that equity, after deducting goodwill, must be at least 50 per cent of total capital. Additionally within second tier capital general provisions cannot exceed 1.25 per cent of risk assets from 1992, and subordinated debt cannot exceed 50 per cent of first tier capital (that is equity less goodwill).

Annex 1

RISK WEIGHT CATEGORIES: ON BALANCE SHEET

A
0%
- (i) Cash
- (ii) Gold and other bullion held in own vaults or on an allocated basis.
- (iii) Loans to OECD central governments and central banks.
- (iv) Claims collateralised by cash or guaranteed by OECD central governments and central banks.
- (v) Loans to non-OECD central governments and central banks denominated in local currency and funded in that currency.
- (vi) Loans guaranteed by non-OECD central governments or central banks where denominated in local currency and funded in that currency.
- (vii) Certificates of tax deposit.

B
10%
- (i) Loans to discount houses, gilt-edged market-makers, institutions with a money market dealing relationship with the Bank of England, and those Stock Exchange money brokers which operate in the gilt-edged market, where the loans are secured on gilts, UK Treasury bills, eligible local authority and eligible bank bills or London CDs.
- (ii) Holdings of fixed-interest securities issued by OECD central governments with a residual maturity of up to 1 year and floating rate OECD central government securities of any maturity.
- (iii) Claims collateralised by OECD central government fixed-interest securities of up to 1 year, or similar floating-rate securities of any maturity.

(iv) Holdings of non-OECD central government securities with a residual maturity of up to 1 year denominated in local currency and funded by liabilities in the same currency.

C
20%
(i) Holdings of OECD central government fixed-interest securities of a residual maturity of 1 year and over or claims collateralised by such securities.

(ii) Holdings of non-OECD central government secuirities of a maturity of 1 year and over denominated in local currency and funded by liabilities in the same currency.

(iii) Claims on multilateral development banks – IBRD (including IFC), IADB, AsDB, AfDB, EIB and CDB – and claims guaranteed by or collateralised by the securities issued by these institutions.

(iv) Claims on banks incorporated in the OECD and exposures guaranteed (or accepted) by OECD incorporated banks (as before, UK building societies are treated as banks for capital adequacy purposes).

(v) Claims in gold and other bullion on those market-making members of the London Bullion Market Association which are not included in (iv) above.

(vi) Claims on banks incorporated outside the OECD with a residual maturity of up to 1 year and loans of the same maturity guaranteed by non-OECD banks.

(vii) Claims on OECD public sector entities (PSEs) and loans guaranteed by such entities. In the UK PSEs are defined as local authorities and other non-commercial public corporations.

(viii) Loans to discount houses which are unsecured or secured on assets other than specified in B(i) above.

(ix) Cash items in the process of collection.

D
50%
(i) Loans to individuals and to housing associations registered with the Housing Corporation for the sole purpose of residential occupation, fully secured by a first equitable or legal charge.

(ii) Holdings of securities issued by special purpose mortgage finance vehicles where the risk to the security holders is fully and specifically secured against residential mortgage loans which would themselves qualify for the 50 per cent weight, or by assets which qualify for a weight of less than 50 per cent.

(iii) Mortgage sub-participations, where the risk to the sub-participating bank is fully and specifically secured against residential mortgage loans which would themselves qualify for the 50 per cent weight.

E
100%
(i) Claims on the non-bank private sector.

(ii) Claims on banks incorporated outside the OECD with a residual maturity of 1 year and over.

(iii) Claims on central governments outside the OECD (unless denominated in the national currency and funded in that currency).

(iv) Loans guaranteed by claims on non-OECD central governments or central banks, which are not denominated in local currency and funded locally.

(v) Claims on commercial companies owned by the public sector.

(vi) Claims on public sector entities outside the OECD.

(vii) Premises, plant, equipment and other fixed assets.

(viii) Real estate, trade investments and other assets not otherwise specified.

(ix) Aggregate net short open foreign-exchange position.

Annex 2

CREDIT CONVERSION FACTORS: CONVENTIONAL CONTINGENTS

Credit conversion factors should be multiplied by the weights applicable to the category of the counter party for an on balance sheet transaction.

	Instruments	Credit conversion factor (%)
A	Direct credit substitutes, including general guarantees of indebtedness, standby letters of credit serving as financial guarantees, and acceptances	100
B	Sale and repurchase agreements and asset sales with recourse where the credit risk remains with the bank	100
C	Forward asset purchases, forward forward deposits and the unpaid part of partly paid shares and securities, which represent commitments with a certain drawdown	100
D	Transaction-related contingent items, e.g. performance bonds, bid bonds, warranties and standby letters of credit related to particular transactions	50
E	Short-term self-liquidating trade-related contingent items, such as documentary credits collateralised by the underlying shipments	20
F	Note issuance facilities and revolving underwriting facilities	50
G	Other commitments (e.g. formal standby facilities and credit lines) with an original maturity of 1 year and over	50
H	Similar commitments with an original maturity of up to 1 year, or which can be unconditionally cancelled at any time	0
I	Endorsement of bills which have been accepted by a bank	0

Multi-option facilities and other composite products should be disaggregated into their component parts, e.g. into a credit commitment, NIF, etc., and each component part weighted according to the above classification. However, components carrying the lowest credit conversion factors should be disregarded to the extent necessary to ensure that the total value of all the components does not exceed the value of the facility.

7

THE BASIC BANKING MODEL

7.1 Equity Flows or Cashflows?

Chapter 5 covered the ground of traditional cashflow analysis. This chapter shows that much of the conventional approach has, on the face of it, to be abandoned when banking is considered.

It has been suggested that problems in specifying the timing of loan principal repayments could be circumvented by using the weighted cost of capital and what might be termed gross cashflows. Using gross cashflows, however, at least in the literal sense, would be pretty meaningless in a banking context. If deposits are included, then something like 90 per cent of capital is represented by deposits, yet the yields on the assets these deposits help fund, and the interest paid on the deposits, are much of what banking is about. Hiding deposit costs within the weighted cost of capital would result in cashflow or profit figures that are meaningless for a banker. Returns on investments generated by DCF analysis must be capable of being related to everyday management accounts; most bankers think in terms of a return on equity, or of margins on lending, with the latter derived from the required return on equity.

Equity plays a pivotal role in the supervisory constraints imposed. This naturally and inevitably leads to the use of a direct equity measure of cashflows.

There is also another reason for using equity flows which is both pragmatic and conceptual. In Chapter 5 the weighted cost of capital only gave the required return to shareholders and lenders under very specific and limited circumstances. Both shareholders and lenders had to have their principal repaid in proportion to economic depreciation. The debt structure of banks, however, is determined by the way they manage their balance sheets, which reflects the capital adequacy constraints and liquidity requirements they must satisfy. Effectively banks do not repay their borrowings, they are simply rolled over or one set of term borrow-

FINANCIAL DECISION-MAKING

ings is replaced by another. Equity flows automatically reflect the interest payments a bank's liability structure imposes upon it.

7.2 Back to Accounting Profits

The equity constraints imposed upon banks are wholly based on the equity shown in their audited accounts, though certain items, such as property revaluation reserves, are excluded. For the DCF specialist this has strange consequences. For example, conventional depreciation charges are arbitrary, having little to do with economic reality, yet bank supervisors doggedly ignore economic fundamentals and happily accept the accountants' conventions. The implication is inescapable – depreciation is a deduction from book equity, and reduces the equity measure used to judge capital adequacy. If the level of risk-weighted assets is to be maintained, the depletion in book equity must be made good; and this can only be done through an injection of equity by shareholders or by a reduction in dividends. Alternatively the bank's assets must be reduced. As far as the bank's shareholders are concerned, the depreciation charge is an equity outflow, and it must be replaced (see Chapter 12.2, which considers the evaluation of fixed assets).

After all that has gone before, the corollary is quite startling. All deductions from and additions to accounting profits are deductions from or additions to shareholders' equity as shown in a bank's accounts. As such, they must be deducted from or added to the equity flows that are discounted by the bank's COE. What this really says is that traditional cashflow concepts are otiose in a banking context. Only accounting profits are relevant, since, apart from any equity injections, they completely determine what is or is not available to shareholders. Other examples from Chapter 5 can be taken to further illustrate this approach. Changes in creditors, representing changes in unpaid for purchases, are excluded from cashflow analysis, but hit the profit and loss account. Therefore they are deductions from the equity flows, since they must be made good if asset levels are to be maintained. Nevertheless the bank does benefit, and the benefit is included in profits. Increased creditors are a balance sheet liability exactly offset by assets on the other side of the balance sheet. These assets generate income and hence profits, as do delays in the payment of corporation taxes.

On the other side, increased debtors reflect income due but unpaid, and this income is included in book profits and is therefore available for dividend payments. Debtors nevertheless have an adverse impact on

The Basic Banking Model

profits through the balance sheet. As an asset they have to be financed on the liabilities side of the balance sheet and interest must be paid on the deposits providing the finance. In addition equity and capital are required to support debtors, which will usually have a risk weighting of 1.0.

7.3 A Basic Equity Flow Model

The basics of the equity flow model are illustrated in Table 7.1. In this model initial assets of 100, growing at 10 per cent a year, yield 6 per cent each year. The equity required to support the assets is 10 per cent (for the time being second tier capital is ignored). At the start of year 1 deposits which cost 5 per cent a year are 90, and they then grow in line with assets. At the end of the first year profits are £1.5m, providing a 15 per cent return on opening equity. Everything grows at 10 per cent, so that the return on book equity stays at 15 per cent each year.

Shareholders have to provide £10m to support the initial asset level. By the end of the first year assets are £110m, so that supporting equity must

TABLE 7.1 Equity Flow Model (£m)

Year	0	1	2	3
Opening assets		100.00	110.00	121.000
Opening liabilities				
Equity		10.00	11.00	12.100
Deposits		90.00	99.00	108.900
		100.00	110.00	121.000
Year-end profit and loss				
Yield on assets		6.00	6.60	7.260
Cost of deposits		(4.50)	(4.95)	(5.445)
Profit year end		1.50	1.65	1.815
Equity flows				
Year-end profits		1.50	1.65	1.815
Equity	(10.00)	(1.00)	(1.10)	12.100
Equity flows	(10.00)	0.50	0.55	13.915
Discounted equity flows	(10.00)	0.4348	0.4159	9.1493
Accounting return		15%	15%	15%

[69]

FINANCIAL DECISION-MAKING

increase to £11m. Increased equity of £1m has to come from somewhere, and in practice it comes from retained earnings, so at the end of year 1 only £0.5m can be paid in dividends, and this is year 1's equity flow. Similarly year 2's equity flow is £0.55m, which not surprisingly is up 10 per cent on the previous year's. At the end of year 3 the bank is sold for book value – £12.1m, the sum of the annual equity injections. Therefore the final cashflow consists of profits plus the bank's book value, or net worth, and the total amount can be distributed to shareholders.

Not surprisingly, discounting the equity flows at 15 per cent generates a zero NPV. The initial equity flow or dividend is 5 per cent of the initial equity outlay, while the equity flows and the bank's equity are growing at 10 per cent p.a. As shown in Chapter 2, this must result in a 15 per cent IRR. However, the equality of annual book returns on equity and the IRR only results from the simplicity of the assumptions made. In any realistic environment this will not happen.

7.4 Accounting Profits and Cashflows Revisited

Now that the equity flow model has been introduced, the differences in conventional cashflow analysis and the methodology adopted here can be illustrated, by the example shown in Table 7.2. To start off, a bank lends £100m against deposits of £90m and supporting equity of £10m. Profits are £3m a year, but there are debtors of £3m at year end, reflecting the assumption that £3m of income has not been received. Thus income received (row 11) is only £9m. In the first year therefore the bank has profits of £3m, but has an operational cashflow of zero (row 13).

It can only pay away its profits as dividends by borrowing £3m to finance the debtors (row 14). Debtors, however, have a risk weighting of 1.0 and need £0.3m of equity support, so that in year 2 opening equity increases to £10.3m. The extra £0.3m of equity required is shown as incremental equity in rows 9 and 16. As described in the previous section, equity flows are derived by deducting incremental equity from profits, so year 1's equity flow is £2.7m.

The flow of cash coming into the bank, after borrowing £3m, is the £3m shown in row 15. Of this cash inflow, £0.3m is retained to fund the additional requirement of equity, so that £2.7m is available to pay dividends. Hence the equity flows derived from profits and those derived from the cashflow statement equate.

In year 2 the income owed from the previous year is paid, and this offsets debtors outstanding at year end. Hence income received is £12m

The Basic Banking Model

TABLE 7.2 Profits and Cashflow (£m)

	Year	0	1	2	3	4
	Opening assets					
1	Lending		100.00	100.00	100.00	100.00
2	Debtors			3.00	3.00	3.00
			100.00	103.00	103.00	103.00
	Opening liabilities					
3	Equity		10.00	10.30	10.30	10.30
4	Deposits		90.00	89.70	89.70	89.70
5	Borrowing			3.00	3.00	3.00
			100.00	103.00	103.00	103.00
	Profit and Loss Account					
6	Income (at 12% of assets)		12.00	12.00	12.00	12.00
7	Costs (at 10% of funds)		(9.00)	(9.27)	(9.27)	(9.27)
8	Profit		3.00	2.73	2.73	2.73
9	Incremental Equity	(10)	(0.3)			10.30
10	Equity Flows	(10)	2.7	2.73	2.73	13.03
	IRR	27.7%				
	Cashflows					
11	Income received		9.00	12.00	12.00	12.00
12	Costs		(9.00)	(9.27)	(9.27)	(9.27)
13	Operational cashflow		0.00	2.73	2.73	2.73
14	Additional borrowing		3.00			
15	Cash inflow		3.00	2.73	2.73	2.73
16	Incremental equity	(10)	(0.30)			10.30
17	Equity flows	(10)	2.7	2.73	2.73	13.03
	Conventional cashflows					
18	Income		9	12	12	12
19	Costs		9	9	9	9
			–	3	3	3
20	Incremental equity	(10)	0	0	0	13
21	Cashflow	(10)	0	3	3	16
	IRR	25%				

(line 11), the same as the profit and loss figure (row 6). Deposits plus borrowings have increased to £92.7m, so that at 10 per cent they cost

FINANCIAL DECISION-MAKING

£9.27m. Both profits (row 8) and operational cashflow (row 13) are the same; likewise for year 3.

In year 4 profits remain at £2.73m. At year end the bank is sold for its book value of £10.3m (row 9), and the equity flow is £13.03m (row 10). At the end of year 4 £3m is still owing, but, due to the payment of £3m owing from year 3, income is still £12m. With costs at £9.27m the operational cashflow is £2.73m. The income from sale, shown in row 16, is £10.3m, so that the cash inflow is £13.03. Again this squares with the equity flow calculated from profits.

Thus both approaches to equity flows give the same results. However, the cashflow statement derived above is not the conventional one used in DCF analysis. A conventional approach to cashflows, though one treating interest on deposits as a cost, is shown at the end of the table. As with the previous case, there is an initial equity injection of £10m to support the bank's lending, but in year 1 conventional cashflow analysis would exclude the possibility of borrowing. The net cash inflow is therefore zero, and by implication so are dividends.

As no dividends are paid, there is no need to borrow to fund the debtors, and equity increases to £13m. In years 2 and 3 income is £12m and costs are £9m, so that the operational cashflow is £3m. The final year's operational cashflow is still £3m and book equity is £13m, which is the price received on sale to give a total cashflow of £16m. The IRR using this approach is 25 per cent compared to the 27.7 per cent when actual dividend payments are discounted.

7.5 Opportunity Costs

Most banks of any size consist of a holding or parent company, various subsidiaries and divisions. Although few if any of these subsidiaries and divisions will have the same capital structure as the parent bank, their assets must also be backed by the required amount of capital. This key aspect of the banking model is now dealt with.

Consider a bank which initially has no subsidiaries. Its assets, taken to equal RWA, are £100m, supported by £10m of equity. The balance sheets of this bank are shown in Table 7.3.

Assume that the bank's COE is r, and that deposits cost i. The yield on assets y must satisfy the following relation:

$$100y = 10r + 90i \quad\quad\quad\quad\quad\quad\quad\quad\quad\quad\quad (7.1)$$

The Basic Banking Model

TABLE 7.3 Cost of Equity and Yield on Assets

	Group	Parent	Sub.		Group	Parent	Sub.
Equity	10	10	–	Assets	100	100	–
Deposits	90	90	–	Subsidiary	–	–	–
	100	100	–		100	100	–

that is, total income must be sufficient to cover the cost of deposits (i.e. $90i$), and remunerate equity at a rate r (i.e. $10r$).

Equation 7.1 can be rewritten:

$$100y = 10(r-i) + 100i$$

that is:

$$y = \frac{10}{100}(r - i) + i \qquad (7.2)$$

where 10/100 is the equity ratio. Thus the required margin, defined as required yield less the interest rate on deposits, is the equity ratio multiplied by $(r-i)$.

Next the bank decides to set up a subsidiary, but does not go to its shareholders for more equity. Hence the subsidiary's assets must be matched by a decline in the holding company's assets (remembering assets are taken to equal RWAs). It is further assumed that the parent's assets generate sufficient income for it to earn its COE. The situation is shown in Table 7.4.

As a result of the investment the parent company's assets have to fall by £20m to offset the subsidiary's assets. At the same time it has

TABLE 7.4 Opportunity Cost of Subsidiary (£m)

	Group	Parent	Sub.		Group	Parent	Sub.
Equity	10	10	3	Assets	100	80	20
Deposits	90	73	17	Subsidiary	–	3	–
	100	83	20		100	83	20

[73]

endowed its subsidiary with £3m of equity, so that the subsidiary's deposits are £17m. Since consolidated deposits are £90m, the parent's own deposit falls to 73. The cost of the investment to the parent is:

- The yield forgone on assets of £20m, less
- The interest saved on reduced deposits of £17m.

Equation 7.2 gives the yield on the assets forgone. Applying this yield to the £20m reduction in assets and allowing for interest saved, gives:

$$20[0.1(r-i) + i] - 17i$$

that is:

$$2(r-i) + 3i \hspace{2cm} (7.3)$$

In other words, the investment in the subsidiary is only worthwhile if its profits are at least equal to 7.3. More generally it can be stated that the subsidiary's profits must at least equal:

(Equity imputed to subsidiary)$(r-i)$ + (Equity endowed in subsidiary)i

The equity needed to support the subsidiary's assets of £20m (to be called 'imputed equity' or IE for brevity) must, just like any other equity invested in the bank, earn r, the cost of equity. However, this cost is partly offset as equity replaces deposits and saves the bank their cost. The holding company endows its subsidiary with equity, but has to borrow to do this, and its interest payments correspondingly increase.

One of the most important relations in this book has been derived and can be formally written as:

$$SP \geq IE(r-i) + EEi \hspace{2cm} (7.4)$$

The sign $\geq$ denotes greater than or equal to, and the symbols used are:

SP is the subsidiary's profits, IE the imputed equity, EE the endowed equity, r the COE, and i the cost of deposits.

Expression 7.4 can be rewritten:

$$SP \geq IEr - IEi + EEi$$

that is:

$$SP + IEi - EEi \geq IEr \quad\quad\quad (7.5)$$

The LHS of this equation is called the 'adjusted profits'.

In Chapter 2 it was shown that a sum S invested at an interest rate r had a zero PV when discounted at r. That is:

$$-S + \frac{Sr}{(1+r)} + \frac{Sr}{(1+r)^2} + \ldots + \frac{Sr + S}{(1+r)^n} = 0$$

Assume the sum invested is the imputed equity needed to support increased banking assets. The above expression then becomes:

$$-IE + \frac{IEr}{(1+r)} + \frac{IEr}{(1+r)^2} + \ldots + \frac{IEr + IE}{(1+r)^n} = 0 \quad\quad (7.6)$$

Using 7.5, the term IEr can be replaced by $SP + (IE - EE)i$, in which case equation 7.6 becomes:

$$-IE + \frac{SP + (IE-EE)i}{(1+r)} + \frac{SP + (IE-EE)i}{(1+r)^2} + \ldots +$$

$$\frac{SP + (IE-EE)i + IE}{(1+r)^n} \geq 0 \quad\quad\quad (7.7)$$

This relation is the most fundamental one in the book. It states that the investment in the subsidiary is worthwhile when the discounted value of the adjusted profits, plus the discounted repayment (or release) of the imputed equity, is greater than zero. While various modifications will be made to 7.7, it remains the basis of all that follows.

7.6 Equity Injections

The results obtained in the previous section still hold if the subsidiary's £20m of assets are supported by additional equity rather than a run-down in the parent's assets. Under these circumstances Table 7.4 is revised as Table 7.5.

FINANCIAL DECISION-MAKING

TABLE 7.5 Direct Equity Cost of Subsidiary (£m)

	Group	Parent	Sub.		Group	Parent	Sub.
Equity	12	12	3	Assets	120	100	20
Deposits	108	91	17	Subsidiary	–	3	–
	120	103	20		120	103	20

Compared with Table 7.3, group assets have increased £20m, equity has necessarily increased £2m and deposits have therefore increased £18m. The cost of supporting the subsidiary's assets becomes the return required on the extra equity of £2m, plus the cost of the parent's increased deposits of £1m, compared to the original £90m shown in Table 7.3. Thus the subsidiary's profits must be at least $2r + i$. This can be rewritten as $2(r-i) + 3i$, which is the same as expression 7.3.

7.7 Second Tier Capital

So far the exposition has ignored second tier capital, by assuming risk-weighted assets are only supported by equity. It is now time to put aside this simplification. Table 7.5 is replaced by one incorporating second tier capital.

The yield on assets has to cover the return on equity, the cost of second tier capital and the cost of deposits. Therefore the yield on assets, y, is derived from the following relation:

$$100y = 6r + 4(i + di) + 90i \qquad (7.8)$$

TABLE 7.6 Asset Yields with Second Tier Capital

	Group	Parent	Sub.		Group	Parent	Sub.
Equity	6	6	–	Assets	100	100	–
Second tier	4	4	–	Subsidiary	–	–	–
Capital	10	10	–				
Deposits	90	90	–				
	100	100	–		100	100	–

[76]

The Basic Banking Model

The expression di denotes the difference between the interest charged on second tier capital and the interest charged on deposits. Equation 7.8 can be rewritten:

$$100y = 6(r - i) + 100i + 4di$$

that is:

$$y = \frac{6}{100}(r - i) + i + \frac{4di}{100} \quad \quad (7.9)$$

where 6/100 is the new imputed equity to RWA's ratio, and 4/100 is the second tier to RWA's ratio. More generally equation (7.9) can be written:

$$y = IE(R)(r-i) + i + T2(R)di \quad \quad (7.10)$$

where IE(R) is the imputed equity to RWA's ratio (equalling 0.06 in this example), and T2(R) = second tier capital to RWA's ratio (equalling 0.04 in this example).

7.8 Opportunity Costs with Second Tier Capital

Tables 7.3 and 7.5 are now revised with first and second tier capital replacing equity capital. In Tables 7.3 and 7.5 the only changes are the replacements of equities of £10m and £12m respectively by:

	£m	
Equity	6.0	7.2
Second tier	4.0	4.8
Total Capital	10.0	12.0

In the latter case the cost of supporting the subsidiary now becomes the return required on the extra equity of £1.2m, and interest on the extra second tier capital of £0.8m. As before, the parent's extra deposits of £1m need to be remunerated. More formally the cost to the parent of establishing the subsidiary becomes:

$$1.2r + 0.8(i + di) + i$$

[77]

FINANCIAL DECISION-MAKING

which can be rewritten:

$$1.2(r-i) + 3i + 0.8di \qquad (7.11)$$

and on generalising is:

$$IE(r-i) + EEi + IE\frac{[T2]di}{[IE]} \qquad (7.12)$$

where T2/IE is the ratio of second tier capital to equity. Apart from the last term containing di, this is the same relationship as expression 7.4, except that the imputed equity ratio has fallen from 0.10 to 0.06.

The relation 7.12 still holds when total capital remains constant, and the parent company's assets have to be reduced to accommodate the subsidiary's assets. This can be confirmed by using equation 7.10 for the yield on the parent's forgone assets, and following the procedure set out in section 7.5.

7.9 Treatment of Second Tier Capital

As an example, a bank's capital structure might be made up as follows:

	£m	Per cent of RWA
Equity	50.0	5.00
Subordinated debt	25.0	2.50
Perpetual floating rate notes	7.5	0.75
General provisions	7.5	0.75
Property revaluation reserves	10.0	1.00
	100.0	10.00

These ratios could be used to calculate the average cost of second tier capital. The result could then be used in expression 7.12. While this approach seems plausible, it is nonetheless erroneous. The current structure of the balance sheet does not reflect how growth in the balance sheet will be supported. Thus if the market will not accept further perpetual floating rate notes, they cannot make any contribution to the capital needed to underwrite the increased assets. Furthermore general provisions actually incur a very heavy cost, since they represent a deduction from the bank's equity base.

The Basic Banking Model

An example clarifies some of these points. Suppose the bank is planning to expand its banking assets by £100m, and that it will not be able to support the increase by FRNs. No extra property will be involved, so that there will be no revaluation reserves now, or in the future, to be taken into second tier capital. Only equity, subordinated debt and general provisions will be available. Balance sheets before and after the creation of the general provision are shown in Table 7.7.

TABLE 7.7   Balance Sheets before General Provision (£m)

Equity	7.0	Banking assets	100
Subordinated debt	3.0		
Total capital	10.0		
Deposits	90.0		
	100.0		100

Balance Sheet after General Provision (£m)

Equity	6.0	Banking assets	99
General provision	1.0	General provision	1
Subordinated debt	3.0		
Total capital	10.0		
Deposits	90.0		
	100.0		100

Before the creation of the general provision, the bank's assets are supported by £7m of equity and £3m of subordinated debt. After the creation of the provision, equity, as defined by BIS, falls to £6m. As subordinated debt cannot exceed 50 per cent of equity, as defined by BIS, the former cannot exceed £3m. The general provision counts as second tier capital, so that after its creation total capital remains £10m. In effect all that has happened is a reclassification of the bank's original equity.

Although the bank's books now show equity of £6m, the true or original equity cost was £7m. Thus for the calculation of required yields, and the amount of equity needed to support a bank's assets, the imputed equity ratio should be taken as 7 per cent. Alternatively, general provisions should be treated as having the same cost as equity. However, the maximum amount of subordinated debt must be calculated in relation to book equity, and in this example it cannot exceed £3m. Likewise, total second tier capital cannot exceed £6m, assuming that it is available.

[79]

FINANCIAL DECISION-MAKING

Banks, it is thought, cannot do away with general provisions, as the market expects to see a level sufficient to provide a safety net against contingencies. On the other hand, there really appears no need, under the BIS rules, to convert any equity to general provisions. Moreover the market may not require a combined equity and general provision ratio of 7 per cent. It may only look for 6 per cent, though under the BIS constraints the bank may not be able to go as low as this. However, in this particular example it could reduce its equity ratio to 6.67 per cent if no general provision is made. The overall 10 per cent capital ratio would be made up by subordinated debt of 3.33 per cent. Since the market is unlikely to require such a high equity plus general provision ratio, banks would be better off eschewing general provisions, and showing higher levels of book equity.

Turning to the other extreme, it is possible that the bank has second tier capital in excess of its equity. If so, such surplus secondary capital can be allocated to other projects. In these circumstances the equity ratio would be lower than a ratio derived on a purely incremental basis.

For the time being the treatment of revaluation reserves will be ignored. Most of Chapter 12 is devoted to this topic.

7.10 Free Funding

In practice the parent company will have various sources of free funds, such as tax and other creditors, available to it. Inclusion of these makes no difference to the opportunity costs of setting up a subsidiary, as Table 7.8 illustrates.

TABLE 7.8 Balance Sheets before Subsidiary (£m)

	Group	Parent	Sub.		Group	Parent	Sub.
Equity	6	6	–	Assets	100	100	–
Second tier	4	4	–	Subsidiary	–	–	–
Capital	10	10	–				
Deposits	80	80	–				
Creditors	10	10	–				
	100	100	–		100	100	–

The Basic Banking Model

	Balance Sheets following Subsidiary (£m)						
	Group	Parent	Sub.		Group	Parent	Sub.
Equity	7.2	7.2	3.0	Assets	120.0	100.0	20.0
Second tier	4.8	4.8	–	Subsidiary	–	3.0	
Total Capital	12.0	12.0	3.0				
Deposits	97.0	81.0	16.0				
Creditors	11.0	10.0	1.0				
	120.0	103.0	20.0		120.0	103.0	20.0

The extra equity and second tier capital are £1.2m and £0.8m respectively, while the parent needs extra deposits of £1m. Therefore the opportunity cost of investing in the subsidiary is unchanged at:

$$1.2(r-i) + 3i + 0.8di$$

which can be confirmed by referring back to expression 7.11.

7.11 Risk-weighted Assets

So far it has been assumed that assets equal RWAs, which means that the former all have a risk weighting of 1.0. If, for example, they had a risk weighting of 0.50, nothing that has gone before changes in any essentials; all that happens is that the required amount of imputed equity and second tier capital falls by a half. Consequently the imputed equity and second tier capital ratios fall by a half. The adjustments for endowed equity and the differential cost of second tier capital remain unchanged. It is left as an exercise for the reader to confirm this.

7.12 An Example

At last a promise can be fulfilled. All the previous work, especially this chapter's, is put together in an example culled from a number of actual evaluations. The data are shown in Table 7.9.

The model could hardly be simpler. Imputed and endowed equity

FINANCIAL DECISION-MAKING

TABLE 7.9 The Equity Flow Model: an Example

		1988	1989	1990	1991	1992	1993	1994	1995	1996	1997	1998	1999	2000	2001	2002
1	Imputed equity	124.6	140.9	149.5	159.5	169.1	179.2	190.0	201.4	213.4	226.3	239.8	254.2	269.5	285.6	302.8
2	Endowed equity	168.0	136.0	170.0	203.0	215.2	228.1	241.8	256.3	271.7	288.0	305.2	323.6	343.0	363.5	385.4
3	Total income	162.0	172.7	188.1	210.0	222.6	236.0	250.1	265.1	281.0	297.9	315.8	334.7	354.8	376.1	398.6
4	Provisions	(0.6)	(0.7)	(0.7)	(0.8)	(0.8)	(0.9)	(1.0)	(1.0)	(1.1)	(1.1)	(1.2)	(1.3)	(1.4)	(1.4)	(1.5)
5	Income less prov.	161.4	172.0	187.4	209.2	221.8	235.1	249.2	264.1	280.0	296.8	314.6	333.4	353.4	374.6	397.1
6	Total costs	(189.1)	(145.5)	(153.5)	(159.5)	(168.2)	(177.2)	(187.8)	(199.1)	(211.0)	(223.7)	(237.1)	(251.3)	(266.4)	(282.4)	(299.4)
7	PBT	(27.7)	26.5	33.9	49.7	53.6	57.9	61.3	65.0	68.9	73.1	77.4	82.1	87.0	92.2	97.8
8	Tax at 0.35	9.7	(9.3)	(11.9)	(17.4)	(18.8)	(20.3)	(21.5)	(22.8)	(24.1)	(25.6)	(27.1)	(28.7)	(30.5)	(32.3)	(34.2)
9	Earnings	(18.0)	7.2	22.0	32.3	34.8	37.6	39.9	42.3	44.8	47.5	50.3	53.4	56.6	59.9	63.5
10	Earnings	(18.0)	7.2	22.0	32.3	34.8	37.6	39.9	42.3	44.8	47.5	50.3	53.4	56.6	59.9	63.5
11	Imputed equity	(16.3)	(8.6)	(10.0)	(9.6)	(10.1)	(10.8)	(11.4)	(12.1)	(12.8)	(13.6)	(14.4)	(15.3)	(16.2)	(17.1)	(302.8)
12	Imputed equity int.	8.1	9.2	9.7	10.4	11.0	11.6	12.3	13.1	13.9	14.7	15.6	16.5	17.5	18.6	19.7
13	Endowed equity int.	(10.9)	(8.8)	(11.1)	(13.2)	(14.0)	(14.8)	(15.7)	(16.7)	(17.7)	(18.7)	(19.8)	(21.0)	(22.3)	(23.6)	(25.0)
14	Second tier adj.	(0.3)	(0.3)	(0.3)	(0.3)	(0.4)	(0.4)	(0.4)	(0.4)	(0.5)	(0.5)	(0.5)	(0.6)	(0.6)	(0.6)	(0.7)
15	Equity flows	(124.6)	(37.4)	8.6	10.4	19.6	21.3	23.3	24.7	26.2	27.7	29.4	31.2	33.0	35.0	37.1	360.3

UK cost of funds 0.10
UK tax less 1 0.65
NPV at 0.14 1.8
IRR 0.1415

[82]

The Basic Banking Model

have been supplied as input, as has the profit and loss account. Usually evaluations are done over a 25-year period, but here it is done over 15 years simply to save space. Specific forecasts are made for the first 5 years, and costs and revenues, imputed and endowed equity are then escalated at appropriate rates.

Rows 1 and 2 show estimated levels of imputed and endowed equity. From 1993 onwards all assets and contingents are assumed to grow at 6 per cent p.a. Therefore imputed equity also grows at the same rate. With constant margins assumed, income also grows at 6 per cent p.a. In this particular case costs are escalated at 6 per cent p.a. from 1993.

All profits and all balance items grow at the same rate from 1993, including endowed equity. If endowed equity grew at any other rate, this would be inconsistent with maintaining a given balance sheet structure and the profit growth assumptions. If follows that profits in excess of the annual increments in endowed equity are remitted to the parent company. Lines 3 to 9 simply summarise the profit and loss account.

The core of the model lies in rows 10 to 14. The first of these rows just shows annual post-tax profits or earnings. Next come the imputed equity flows. Opening imputed equity is £124.6m, and this is the initial outflow of equity. At the beginning of 1989 total imputed equity is £140.9m, giving an increase of £16.3m. This additional equity is a cost to the bank and is shown as an equity outflow, as it is also for the years 1989 to 2001. At the end of 2002 it is assumed that the subsidiary is sold, or wound up, without any gains or losses. As a result £302.8m of equity is released, either to pay as dividends or to support other bank activities.

The imputed equity interest credit is calculated using the bank's cost of funds net of tax, which is taken to be 6.5 per cent, and a similar calculation is made for the endowed equity debit. Line 14 shows the adjustments needed to take account of the differential cost of second tier capital. It is assumed that it is 0.5 per cent more than the cost of funds, and that the second tier to equity ratio for the bank is 4 per cent to 6 per cent. On referring to equation 7.12 it is calculated thus, in the first year:

$0.005 \times (1 - \text{tax rate}) \times 4/6 \times IE$

or $0.005 (1-0.35) \times 4/6 \times 124.6$

In practice this adjustment is generally small enough to be ignored.

The resulting equity flows are shown in row 15. When they are discounted at 14 per cent, the NPV is £1.8m and the IRR is 14.1 per cent. Therefore, if the COE is 14 per cent, the proposed subsidiary is worth establishing, and if it is an existing subsidiary, then it appears profitable and worth maintaining. However, an existing business can always be sold, which might be a more attractive option (considered in the next chapter). Moreover if an existing business is not expected to earn 14 per cent, closure could prove to be an even more expensive option. Again this is considered in the next chapter.

7.13 Terminal Values: a Conundrum

7.13.1 Introduction

A problem that occurs in many DCF analyses is estimation of the terminal worth of the business, which, conceptually, should be either the future discounted stream of dividends or the profit on sale. In the previous section it was assumed that the bank was sold for neither profit nor less at the end of year 15. In practice two methods are often used; they are discussed in the following sections.

7.13.2 Dividends in Perpetuity

With this method a view is taken on the trend in dividends, or the trend in dividend contributions that a subsidiary can make to total dividends. In the previous example a view would have to be taken of the profit contributions, or equity flows, from, say, 2002 onwards.

In 2001 the subsidiary's contribution to group equity was £37.1m. The simplest assumption would be that they could be maintained into the indefinite future, and £37.1m could be discounted from 2002 to infinity. An alternative could be to assume that the contributions carry on growing at 6 per cent p.a., and discount this dividend contribution to infinity. Whatever the detailed assumptions, some view has to be taken, and it will inevitably be arbitrary in nature.

7.13.3 Sale of Business

Here one takes a view on the price earnings ratio in the terminal year. The profit on sale, after capital gains tax, is then calculated and added to the final year's equity flow. Guessing a PE ratio 15 years hence is clearly a pretty futile exercise, so a terminal year only 5 to 10 years out is used in

The Basic Banking Model

this method. Even then it is a pretty hazardous exercise. Moreover the outcome of the evaluation will become heavily dependent upon the PE ratio chosen, rather than upon a judgement of income and cost trends.

7.13.4 Recommended Approach

The approach adopted here is something of a compromise. Forecasts should be made in some detail for as far ahead as practical – certainly for a minimum 5 years. For the next 5 years or so detailed forecasting would be spurious. Nevertheless a view on general trends in balance sheet growth, fees, margins and costs can be taken. Thereafter, unless there are good reasons to the contrary, a neutral view can be taken.

Neutrality, it is suggested, means that risk-weighted assets, income and costs grow in line with long-run real national income growth. The latter would then have to be upped to reflect the inflation rate subsumed within the COE. The neutral projection could be carried forward until year 20 or 25, say, when it is probably best to assume that the business can be sold without profit or loss. By this time discounting will have done most of its work, and the results should not be too sensitive to the terminal value assumption.

8

EXTENSIONS OF THE BANKING MODEL

8.1 Introduction

This chapter covers a number of important topics. It shows how to deal with goodwill, minorities and non-consolidated investments in trade subsidiaries, and is rounded off with examples of an acquisition, a closure and a sale.

8.2 Goodwill

Goodwill occurs when the cost of an acquisition exceeds its net worth. Under the BIS rules, goodwill must be deducted from a bank's equity. On acquisition therefore there are in effect two initial sets of imputed equity: firstly, that calculated with reference to the acquiree's RWA, and secondly, the acquiror's net worth reduced by the goodwill. This reduction has to be made good and is an additional equity cost. When the purchase price is less than the acquiree's net worth, the difference enhances the acquiror's net worth. In this case it can be deducted from imputed equity.

A more formal exposition is given in Table 8.1. The original balance sheet needs no explanation. Acquisition comprises the purchase of a bank with £150m of assets and £140m of liabilities. It costs £15m, but the net cost to the shareholders is £14m, which is the cost of the extra imputed equity of £9m, assuming a 6 per cent equity ratio, plus goodwill of £5m, and is derived as follows:

	£m
Purchase price	15
Less acquiree's equity	(10)
	5
Imputed equity	9
	14

Extensions of the Banking Model

TABLE 8.1   Balance Sheets before Acquisition (£m)

	Group	Parent	Sub.		Group	Parent	Sub.
Equity	60	60	–	Assets	1000	1000	–
Second tier	40	40		Subsidiary			
Total capital	100	100					
Deposits	900	900					
	1000	1000			1000	1000	–

Balance Sheets after Acquisition (£m)

	Group	Parent	Sub.		Group	Parent	Sub.
Equity	74	74	10	Assets	1150	1000	150
Goodwill	(5)	(5)		Subsidiary		10	
Second tier	46	46					
Total capital	115	115	10				
Deposits	1035	895	140				
	1150	1010	150		1150	1010	150

This says that although the acquiror's shareholders have initially to provide £15m, this amount is offset by the £10m contributed by the acquiree, which can then be distributed to shareholders or used to support expansion elsewhere in the Group.

Returning to Table 7.9, suppose the projections reflected the forecast position of an acquiree, and that the purchase price is £200m. Since its equity is £168m (row 2), goodwill is £32m. Only one adjustment is required to the equity flows in line 15, i.e. a further deduction of £32m at the beginning of 1988. The initial equity flow becomes −£156.6m instead of −£124.6m, while the NPV becomes −£30.2m and the IRR falls to 12 per cent.

8.3   Minorities

When, for example, 75 per cent of a financial institution is bought, there are still other or minority interests holding 25 per cent of its equity. Generally such an acquisition will be consolidated into the holding company's accounts. Risk-weighted assets will be calculated on the full value of the acquiree's assets – not 75 per cent. Consequently the acquiror will need sufficient equity to support the RWAs it does not own. To offset this, minority interests are included in the acquiror's equity for capital adequacy purposes.

This means that in financial evaluations minority interests in a subsidiary can be deducted from imputed equity in each year. As far as the parent is concerned, its investment in the subsidiary is the latter's total equity less minority interests. This in turn is the value of equity endowed in the subsidiary, and is the sum that should be used in the endowed equity debit adjustment.

8.4 Non-consolidated Investments

Non-consolidated investments in financial subsidiaries are deducted from total capital under the BIS rules. If equity accounts for 60 per cent of total capital, then such an investment needs 60 per cent equity backing, and this ratio applied to the investment gives the amount of imputed equity required to support it. The subsidiary's endowed equity is simply the value of the investment itself.

8.5 A Case Study: an Acquisition

In this example the vendor only provided partial information, but only indicative bids were required. A shortlist of potential buyers was to be drawn up, partly on the basis of the bids, partly on the bidders' competence in the business and partly on their status.

A summary of the information available, along with the evaluation, is shown in Table 8.2. The balance sheet was used to estimate risk-weighted assets and hence imputed equity (rows 1–9). Fixed assets and investments require imputed equity of 0.06, i.e. an IE ratio of 0.06 × a risk weighting of 1.0. Loans to parent and trade investments (assumed to be financial investments) have a 60 per cent weighting, since they have to be fully covered by first tier plus second tier capital.

Cash and short-term funds were assumed to be nearly all deposits with banks. As they have a 0.2 risk weighting, their equity ratio is 1.2 per cent. Investments have a risk weighting of 1.0 and hence an equity ratio of 6 per cent.

Extensions of the Banking Model

TABLE 8.2 An Acquisition

	IE Ratio	Dec. 86	Dec. 87	June 88	Dec. 88	1989	1990	1991	1992	2004	2005	2006	2007	2008
ASSETS														
1 Fixed assets	0.060	0.22	0.29	0.30	0.31	0.31	0.31	0.31	0.31	0.31	0.31	0.31	0.31	0.31
2 Loan to parent	0.600	0.75	0.75	0.75	0.00									
3 Trade investments	0.600	0.08	0.21	0.37	0.37	0.37	0.37	0.37	0.37	0.37	0.37	0.37	0.37	0.37
4 Cash & short-term funds	0.012	9.24	6.16	6.32	6.34	7.30	8.39	9.65	11.10	21.82	22.91	24.06	25.26	26.53
5 Investments	0.060	4.42	4.52	4.63	4.65	4.65	4.65	4.65	4.65	4.65	4.65	4.65	4.65	4.65
6 Advances customers	0.045	2.96	5.73	5.87	5.90	6.78	7.80	8.97	10.32	20.30	21.31	22.38	23.50	24.67
7 Sundry debtors	0.060	1.86	2.40	2.46	2.47	2.84	3.26	3.75	4.32	8.49	8.92	9.36	9.83	10.32
8 Other	0.012				0.75	0.75	0.75	0.75	0.75	0.75	0.75	0.75	0.75	0.75
9 Balancing item	0.012				0.00	(1.42)	(1.11)	(0.69)	(0.20)	2.87	3.14	3.42	3.70	3.99
10 Total assets		19.52	20.05	20.69	20.78	21.57	24.42	27.76	31.60	59.56	62.36	65.29	68.36	71.58
11 Imputed equity		1.13	1.34	1.45	1.02	1.07	1.16	1.26	1.38	2.28	2.37	2.46	2.56	2.67
12 Endowed equity		1.63	2.24	2.60	2.97	1.07	1.16	1.26	1.38	2.28	2.37	2.46	2.56	2.67
LIABILITIES														
13 Equity		1.13	1.74	2.10	2.47	1.07	1.16	1.26	1.38	2.28	2.37	2.46	2.56	2.67
14 Loan stock: 1		0.75	0.75	0.75	0.00	0.00	0.00	0.00	0.00	0.00	0.00	0.00	0.00	0.00
15 Loan stock: 2		0.75	0.75	0.75	0.00	0.00	0.00	0.00	0.00	0.00	0.00	0.00	0.00	0.00
16 Minorities		0.50	0.50	0.50	0.50	0.00	0.00	0.00	0.00	0.00	0.00	0.00	0.00	0.00
17 Deferred tax		0.17	0.25	0.25	0.25	0.25	0.25	0.25	0.25	0.25	0.25	0.25	0.25	0.25
18 Due to customers		15.14	14.39	14.63	14.70	16.90	19.44	22.35	25.70	50.56	53.09	55.74	58.53	61.45
19 Sundry creditors		0.84	1.42	1.45	1.45	1.67	1.92	2.21	2.54	5.00	5.25	5.52	5.79	6.08
20 Dividends		0.07	0.06	0.06	0.00	0.00	0.00	0.00	0.00	0.00	0.00	0.00	0.00	0.00
21 Tax		0.10	0.11	0.11	0.18	0.44	0.42	0.45	0.49	0.23	0.16	0.09	(0.00)	(0.11)
22 Due to parent		0.08	0.09	0.09	0.00	0.00	0.00	0.00	0.00	0.00	0.00	0.00	0.00	0.00
23 Other					1.23	1.23	1.23	1.23	1.23	1.23	1.23	1.23	1.23	1.23
24 Total liabilities		19.52	20.05	20.69	20.78	21.57	24.42	27.76	31.60	59.56	62.36	65.29	68.36	71.58
25 PROFIT AFTER TAX		0.64	0.81	0.37	0.71	0.82	0.77	0.84	0.92	0.43	0.30	0.16	(0.01)	(0.20)
			EQUITY FLOWS											
26 Profit					(1.02)	0.82	0.77	0.84	0.92	0.43	0.30	0.16	(0.01)	(0.20)
27 Imputed equity						(0.06)	(0.09)	(0.10)	(0.12)	(0.09)	(0.09)	(0.10)	(0.10)	2.56
28 IE credit						0.07	0.07	0.08	0.08	0.14	0.15	0.15	0.16	0.17
29 EE credit						(0.19)	(0.07)	(0.08)	(0.08)	(0.14)	(0.15)	(0.15)	(0.16)	(0.17)
30 Equity flows					(1.02)	0.63	0.68	0.74	0.80	0.35	0.21	0.06	(0.11)	2.37
				NPV at	0.14	3.94								

Advances to customers were partly secured by cash. Their average risk weighting was taken as 75 per cent, to give an imputed equity requirement of 4.5 per cent. Sundry debtors have a risk weighting of 1.0, and hence an imputed equity requirement of 6.0 per cent. The loan to the parent was to be repaid at the end of December 1988 (row 2), and it was assumed that it would be deposited with banks which have a 20 per cent risk weighting; it is shown as 'Other' in row 8 with an equity ratio of 1.2 per cent.

Line 9 shows the 'balancing item', which ensures both sides of the balance sheet are equal. When it is negative, it is in fact a liability and the 'income' it generates is negative. When it becomes positive, the balancing item is an asset and the income, taken to be a money market rate, is positive. At this point it also has to be given a risk weighting and an imputed equity ratio. The latter was taken as 1.2 per cent for the same reason as 'Other'.

Minorities have not been deducted from either imputed or endowed equity, as the purchase price included minority interests. From the end of 1989 all the bank's endowed equity in excess of its imputed equity was assumed remitted to its new parent company, which mainly accounts for the relatively large negative balancing item at the end of 1989.

Fee income and operating costs were projected on the basis of judgements about the acquiree's business, and potential synergies with the acquiror. Assets and their yields were dealt with in the same way. After the first 5 years, underlying costs were assumed to escalate more rapidly than income, which explains the projected losses in the last 2 years.

The resultant equity flows are shown in the second half of Table 8.2. The 'second tier' interest adjustments have been excluded, as their impact is negligible. Moreover, apart from 1989, the imputed equity credit and endowed equity debit cancel out, on the assumptions made.

At the end of 1988 the acquiree had a projected book value of £2.97m, including minorities; that is the endowed equity, and any payment in excess of this represents goodwill. As shown in section 8.2 this represents a cost over and above the imputed equity needed to support the acquisition. Thus the following relationship has to hold if the acquisition is to be worthwhile:

Imputed equity + Goodwill ≤ Present value

In this case:

£1.02m + Goodwill ≤ £4.96m

In other words, up to £3.94m can be paid for goodwill. Since the acquiree's book value is £2.97m, including minorities, this means it is worth paying up to £6.90m to make the acquisition.

8.6 Closure

Return to the case illustrated in Table 7.9, but assume that the COE is 20 per cent rather than 14 per cent. The NPV becomes minus £47.8m, and on the basis of this new COE, the subsidiary is clearly unprofitable. Two options are available, closure or sale, neither of which may be worthwhile. The closure case is considered first.

Costless closure is the hard-nosed chief executive's dream. Fortunately for those affected, costs often arise, in three basic forms: redundancy and associated costs, write-off of fixed assets, and additional loan losses. They may be, at least partly, offset by any profits on the sale of any property net of capital gains tax.

Redundancy and associated costs require no explanation. Fixed assets that cannot be sold, or sold only at a loss with respect to book value, have to be written off against the bank's equity. This diminution in the equity base, which has to be made good, is a consequence of closure and must be debited against it; in fact this extra equity has to be used to repay the deposits that could not otherwise be repaid owing to the write-off. Rapid run-down of the business will probably mean that not all loans will be repaid in full. Additional loan losses consequent to closure are clearly costs that should go against it.

Closure cannot occur instantaneously; it has to be managed, and could take up to a year and sometimes longer. In the following example it is assumed to take a year. The situation is summarised in Table 8.3.

Owing to poor morale and general disruption, losses are even higher in 1988 than they otherwise would have been. At the end of 1988 all the imputed equity tied up in the subsidiary is released. Rows 3 to 5 are simply a replication of Table 7.9. Redundancy costs net of tax are estimated at £20m, and additional loan losses net of tax at £10.5m (rows 6 and 7). Net write-offs on fixed assets amount to £18m. On a 20 per cent discount rate, the NPV is (£84.6m). Thus, although carrying on the business is unprofitable, closure is even worse.

FINANCIAL DECISION-MAKING

TABLE 8.3 Closure Equity Flows (£m)

			1988
1	Earnings		(25.0)
2	Imputed equity	(124.6)	124.6
3	Imputed equity interest		8.1
4	Endowed equity interest		(10.9)
5	Second tier adjustment		(0.3)
6	Redundancy costs		(20.0)
7	Loan losses		(10.5)
8	Fixed assets written off		(18.0)
		(124.6)	48.0
NPV at 20% (£84.6m)			

8.7 Sale

Goodwill, when included in an acquisition, imposes an additional equity cost over that of imputed equity. A sale price, net of capital gains tax, in excess of book value is pure bonus, while a price less than book value is pure loss. Table 8.4 illustrates.

Again it is assumed that a year is taken to divest the business successfully; earnings are unchanged. The imputed equity figures were

TABLE 8.4 Equity Flows on Sale (£m)

			1988
1	Earnings		(18.0)
2	Imputed equity	(124.6)	124.6
3	Imputed equity interest		8.1
4	Endowed equity interest		(10.9)
5	Second tier adjustment		(0.3)
6	Sale price less endowed equity (170−136)		34.0
7	Capital gains tax		(5.0)
8	Fixed assets written off		–
		(124.6)	132.5
NPV at 20% (£14.2m)			

Extensions of the Banking Model

explained in the previous example. Again rows 3 to 5 are unchanged. It is assumed that the business can be sold for £170m at the end of 1988, when the subsidiary's book value is projected to be £136m. Therefore the sale will add £34m to the holding company's projected equity base. This equity gain of £34m should be added to the equity flow, but a capital gains tax of £5m should be deducted.

At 20 per cent the NPV of the sale strategy is (£14.2m), still causing a loss, but of the three strategies available – continuation, closure and sale – it causes the holding least harm. Unless there are any overriding reasons to the contrary, sale is the preferred option.

One may wonder why the subsidiary is worth more to another enterprise than to the original parent company. There are at least four possibilities: the new company may simply have better management and be capable of deriving an acceptable return; it may have synergies that are not available to the parent company; it may have a different view of its COE, and discount the subsidiary's earnings at well under 20 per cent; or its management may be unwise, and simply have miscalculated.

9

INTERNATIONAL DIMENSIONS

9.1 Additional Considerations

When foreign investments are considered, various complications have to be taken into account. These include the interest rates to be used, foreign exchange or FX movements, holding gains, remittance taxes, local compared to domestic accounting conventions and local capital adequacy requirements. This chapter shows how all these factors are incorporated into the model.

9.2 Interest Rates

The interest rate for calculating the imputed equity credit should be the sterling rate. Equity supporting the subsidiary's RWAs will be raised in the UK in sterling and so replace sterling deposits. Endowed equity in the subsidiary could be borrowed by the parent either in sterling or local currency. In the latter case interest could come from two sources. Firstly, sterling could be converted to foreign currency at future exchange rates; depending upon FX movements this would involve currency gains or losses. As Section 9.6.2 shows, over a period of time FX movements should cancel any interest savings (or costs) that cheaper foreign interest rates appear to give. Secondly, part of the subsidiary's profits could be used. But again any benefits (or losses) will be offset by the benefits forgone in converting local currency to sterling as the former appreciates. The first option will be assumed, as it makes for easier exposition without having any significant positive or negative consequences for evaluations.

International Dimensions

9.3 Foreign Exchange Movements

At a purely computational level FX movements are easy to deal with. Foreign earnings are converted to sterling at year-end FX rates. Thus foreign profits might be forecast to be USD50m at the end of 1990. The forecast exchange rate could be USD1.5 = £1, in which case sterling profits would be £33.33m. Foreign profits would be converted to sterling profits in this way every year end.

Likewise opening levels of imputed and endowed equity should be converted to sterling at opening FX rates. Increments in imputed equity are calculated by deducting the opening level from the closing level, after they have been converted to sterling at opening and closing FX rates. All this will fully reflect the fact that the consolidated balance sheet is controlled in sterling terms by the Bank of England.

9.4 Holding Gains

Suppose over a year the foreign currency appreciates 10 per cent against sterling. While remaining constant in local currency terms, assets and liabilities will increase 10 per cent in sterling, and since assets exceed liabilities (excluding endowed capital), there will be a net sterling gain. The difference between assets and liabilities will be 10 per cent of endowed capital. The FX-generated increase in the sterling value of endowed capital is called a holding gain. This gain can be incorporated into both the consolidated and the parent company's equity, so that it is available either to support an expansion of RWA or for distribution to shareholders, given the level of RWAs. Consequently, it is a true gain to shareholders and should be added to or, in the case of a depreciating currency, deducted from equity flows. It should be noted, however, that all the holding gain does is offset, in part at least, the additional equity needed to support the increased sterling value of the subsidiary's assets.

9.5 FX Gains and Holding Gains: an Example

In this example the impact of FX movements on both profits and holding gains is examined. See Table 9.1.

Let the above balance sheets at the opening FX rate reflect the position at the beginning of the year. Assume that both the subsidiary and the

FINANCIAL DECISION-MAKING

TABLE 9.1 Impact of Exchange Rate Movements

	Group	Parent	Sub.		Group	Parent	Sub.
Equity	50	50	50	Assets	1000	600	400
Second tier	50	50	—	Subsidiary		50	
Capital	100	100	50				
Deposits	900	550	350				
	1000	650	400		1000	650	400

holding company earn 20 per cent on their imputed equity, and for simplicity that second tier capital and deposits cost the same. Then, using expression 7.4, the foreign operation must earn:

$$20(r-i) + 50i$$

as the imputed equity ratio is 50 to 1000. With deposits costing the parent 5 per cent, the subsidiary's earnings become:

$$20(0.20-0.05) + 50 \times 0.05 = £5.5m$$

The holding company earns a yield on its assets of £600m and pays 5 per cent on its deposits and second tier capital. By equation 7.2 the yield on the parent's assets is:

$$600[IE(R)(r-i)+i] = 600[0.05(0.2 - 0.05) + 0.05]$$

and the cost of its borrowings is 5 per cent of £600m. Hence the parent's profits amount to £4.5m. Consequently total earnings are £10m, to give a 20 per cent return on total equity of £50m. The balance sheets after one year, and assuming no FX movements, are shown in Table 9.2.

At the consolidated or group level equity increases by £10m to £60m as a result of the year's total group earnings, while the subsidiary's equity increases £5.5m to £55.5m. Second tier capital is assumed constant, and the balance sheets are assumed to increase only in line with earnings.

If, instead of FX rates remaining constant, the foreign currency appreciates 10 per cent, the subsidiary's balance sheet, in sterling terms, increases by 10 per cent while the parent's balance sheet remains unchanged apart from the FX adjustments. The position is shown in Table 9.3.

International Dimensions

TABLE 9.2 Impact of Exchange Rate Movements (£m)

	Group	Parent	Sub.		Group	Parent	Sub.
Equity	50.0	50.0	50.0	Assets	1010.0	604.5	405.5
Earnings	10.0	10.0	5.5	Subsidiary		55.5	
Total equity	60.0	60.0	55.5				
Second tier	50.0	50.0	–				
Capital	110.0	110.0	55.5				
Deposits	900.0	550.0	350.0				
	1010.0	660.0	405.5		1010.0	660.0	405.5

TABLE 9.3 Impact of Exchange Rate Movements: Final Act (£m)

	Group	Parent	Sub.		Group	Parent	Sub.
Equity	50.00	50.00	55.00	Assets	1050.55	604.50	446.05
Earnings	10.00	10.00	6.05	Subsidiary		61.05	
FX adjust.	5.55	5.55					
Total equity	65.55	65.55	61.05				
Second tier	50.00	50.00	–				
Capital	115.55	115.55	61.05				
Deposits	935.00	550.00	385.00				
	1050.55	665.55	446.05		1050.55	665.55	446.05

All items on both sides of the subsidiary's balance sheet have increased 10 per cent on conversion to sterling. Thus its endowed equity has increased £5.55m from £55.50m to £61.05m. This increase is shown in the consolidated and parent balance sheets as the FX adjustment and consists of two items:

	Value before FX appreciation	Times 0.1
Subsidiary's original profit	5.5	0.55
Subsidiary's opening endowed equity	50.0	5.00
		5.55

The first item reflects the gain in sterling profits due to the strengthening of the foreign currency in relation to sterling. It is automatically taken into account by the conversion of currency profits into sterling by using the year end FX rate, rather than the opening FX rate. In sterling the parent's beginning of the year investment in its subsidiary amounted to £50m, and the extra £5m resulting from the FX gain on opening endowed equity is incorporated into the group's equity. Hence the holding gain of £5m is available for distribution to shareholders. Admittedly payment of the holding gain to shareholders has to be funded, but this is allowed for in the endowed equity debit as endowed equity increases by the holding gain.

9.6 Consistency of Assumptions

9.6.1 *Inflation*

Conceptually interest, inflation and FX rates should be mutually consistent, at least in the longer term. If prices in the UK increase 5 per cent p.a. while those in the USA remain constant, UK goods will become overpriced in USD terms and sterling will have to depreciate to compensate for this. If a UK product cost £20,000 at the start of the year, and the FX rate was USD2 = £1, then the product would sell for USD40,000 in the States. After a year the sterling cost becomes £21,000, owing to the impact of inflation, and the product is now uncompetitive at USD42,000 and does not sell.

A 5 per cent appreciation of the dollar will correct the situation. The exchange rate becomes USD2.0/1.05 = USD1.9048 = £1. At this rate the dollar cost of the product falls back to its original USD40,000. Equilibrium is restored and British products are once again competitive.

9.6.2 *Interest Rates*

Real and nominal interest rates were discussed in section 3.5, which showed how interest would have to vary with inflation if real purchasing power was to be maintained. As an example, assume that interest rates would be 3 per cent without inflation. After a year a £1000 investment would be worth £1030. With inflation of 5 per cent p.a. the purchasing power of the £1030 would be deflated thus: £1030.00/1.05. In other words it would only be worth £980.95. If interest rates adjust to reflect inflation fully, the £1030 would have to increase to £1030.00 × 1.05, or £1000.00 ×

International Dimensions

1.0815. Interest rates would have to increase from 3 per cent to 8.15 per cent to compensate exactly for inflation.

Exchange rates must also fully reflect differential interest rates. If they did not, it would be cheaper to borrow in currencies with low interest rates. Assume sterling interest rates are 8.15 per cent and dollar rates are 3 per cent, with a constant exchange rate of USD2 = £1. Further assume that a company needs to borrow £1m. At the beginning of the year the company could borrow USD2m and convert them to £1m. Come the end of the year, the company will owe USD2.06m. With FX rates unchanged, the company will only need to find £1.03m to repay the debt. Had it borrowed in sterling, its repayment of principal plus interest would have amounted to £1.0815m. By borrowing in dollars the company saved itself £51,500.

All companies would find such an option worthwhile, but their consequent demand for dollars would push up their price until ultimately no gain was available. Furthermore arbitrage would ensure that dollar borrowing could not be cheaper than sterling borrowing. Arbitrageurs would borrow in dollars and lend in sterling to make large profits at minimal cost. Again the consequent demand for dollars would push up their price.

Equilibrium would only be restored once the dollar had appreciated 5 per cent. After the dollar appreciation the company that had borrowed dollars would still owe USD2.06m at the end of the year. At the new exchange rate of USD1.9048 = £1 the company would have to find £1.0815m to repay its debt, which is exactly the same as the cost of borrowing £1m in sterling at 8.15 per cent interest.

9.6.3 Implications for Project Appraisal

In practice, over any arbitrary period of several years, markets will not be in equilibrium. Forecasts, however unreliable they are, have to be made for a few years ahead. Simply carrying on with current rates is itself a forecast and will often be one of the worst available. At the very least a view should be taken on whether or not FX rates and interest rates are above or below long-term trends. They can then be adjusted to trend over several years.

However the forecasts are made, it would be a delusion to carry on forecasting after 3 to 5 years. All that can be done is to ensure consistency of assumptions. Thus currency movements must reflect both differential interest and inflation rates, and these rates must also be consistent.

FINANCIAL DECISION-MAKING

9.7 Local Accounting v Domestic Accounting

Domestic accounting rules are used by supervisors for control purposes. Accounting rules can differ quite substantially between countries. When one is evaluating a foreign project, one must adjust the local accounting rules to reflect the position that appears in the domestic consolidated and parent company accounts.

A few examples give the flavour of the problem. Provisioning policies will differ: the local rules will have to apply for local tax purposes, but the home rules for domestic earnings and taxation. Depreciation conventions sometimes differ, and again the domestic rules must be used. Property may be at book value locally, but be revalued in the head office books; again the latter should be used.

9.8 An Example

To provide a basis for discussion, the example shown in Table 7.9 has been modified to reflect the international dimensions of the appraisal problem. Up until row 9 nothing changes, but what were sterling figures in Table 7.9 are now currency figures in Table 9.4. Therefore all the figures in Table 9.4 have to be converted to sterling, and the first real change is the insertion of a set of FX rates in row 10.

FX rates have been explicity forecast until the beginning of 1994. Purely illustrative figures have been used to show their impact on equity flows. From the end of 1993 the FX rates reflect differential inflation (rows 11 and 12). As UK inflation is higher than the foreign rate, sterling continuously depreciates from 1994. The inflation rates themselves are constrained to be consistent with interest rates. UK interest is 10 per cent, and the foreign interest rate used in generating currency earnings is 8 per cent. If UK inflation is taken as given, at 5 per cent, then consistency implies that the foreign rate must be $[(1.05 \times 1.08)/1.1] - 1 = .0309$, or 3.09 per cent.

From the FX rates given in row 10 the opening 1988 imputed equity of USD124.6m becomes £62.3m. Likewise USD earnings of USD17.2m in 1989 become sterling earnings of £8.6m, using the year end exchange rate (row 13). At the beginning of 1993 and 1994 the imputed equity figures are:

	1993	1994	Difference
Opening imputed equity : USD	179.2	190.0	10.8
: GBP	89.6	104.5	14.9
FX rates	2.0000	1.8182	

[100]

TABLE 9.4 Appraisal of an International Project

		1988	1989	1990	1991	1992	1993	1994	1995	1996	1997	1998	1999	2000	2001	2002
1	Imputed equity	124.6	140.9	149.5	159.5	169.1	179.2	190.0	201.4	213.4	226.3	239.8	254.2	269.5	285.6	302.8
2	Endowed equity	168.0	136.0	170.0	203.0	215.2	228.1	241.8	256.3	271.7	288.0	305.2	323.6	343.0	363.5	385.4
3	Total income	162.0	172.7	188.1	210.0	222.6	236.0	250.1	265.1	281.0	297.9	315.8	334.7	354.8	376.1	398.6
4	Provisions	(0.6)	(0.7)	(0.7)	(0.8)	(0.8)	(0.9)	(1.0)	(1.0)	(1.1)	(1.1)	(1.2)	(1.3)	(1.4)	(1.4)	(1.5)
5	Income less prov.	161.4	172.0	187.4	209.2	221.8	235.1	249.2	264.1	280.0	296.8	314.6	333.4	353.4	374.6	397.1
6	Total costs	(189.1)	(145.5)	(153.5)	(159.5)	(168.2)	(177.2)	(187.8)	(199.1)	(211.0)	(223.7)	(237.1)	(251.3)	(266.4)	(282.4)	(299.4)
7	PBT	(27.7)	26.5	33.9	49.7	53.6	57.9	61.3	65.0	68.9	73.1	77.4	82.1	87.0	92.2	97.8
8	Tax at 0.35	9.7	(9.3)	(11.9)	(17.4)	(18.8)	(20.3)	(21.5)	(22.8)	(24.1)	(25.6)	(27.1)	(28.7)	(30.5)	(32.3)	(34.2)
9	Currency earnings	(18.0)	17.2	22.0	32.3	34.8	37.6	39.9	42.3	44.8	47.5	50.3	53.4	56.6	59.9	63.5
10	FX year end	2.0000	2.0000	2.0000	2.0000	2.0000	1.8182	1.7851	1.7527	1.7208	1.6895	1.6588	1.6286	1.5990	1.5700	1.5414
11	Foreign inflation		1.0309													
12	UK inflation		1.0500													
	EQUITY FLOWS															
13	Sterling earnings		(9.0)	8.6	11.0	16.2	17.4	20.7	22.3	24.1	26.0	28.1	30.3	32.8	35.4	38.2	41.2
14	Imputed equity	(62.3)	(8.2)	(4.3)	(5.0)	(4.8)	(5.1)	(14.9)	(8.3)	(9.0)	(9.7)	(10.5)	(11.3)	(12.2)	(13.2)	(14.2)	(192.9)
15	Imputed equity int.		4.0	4.6	4.9	5.2	5.5	6.4	6.9	7.5	8.1	8.7	9.4	10.1	11.0	11.8	12.8
16	Endowed equity int.		(5.5)	(4.4)	(5.5)	(6.6)	(7.0)	(8.2)	(8.8)	(9.5)	(10.3)	(11.1)	(12.0)	(12.9)	(13.9)	(15.1)	(16.3)
17	Second tier adj.		(0.1)	(0.2)	(0.2)	(0.2)	(0.2)	(0.2)	(0.2)	(0.2)	(0.3)	(0.3)	(0.3)	(0.3)	(0.4)	(0.4)	(0.4)
18	Holding gain		0.0	0.0	0.0	0.0	0.0	11.4	2.5	2.7	2.9	3.1	3.3	3.6	3.9	4.2	4.5
19	Equity flows	(62.3)	(18.7)	4.3	5.2	9.8	10.7	15.3	14.4	15.5	16.7	18.1	19.5	21.1	22.7	24.6	234.7
	UK cost of funds	0.10															
	UK tax less 1	0.65															
	NPV at	0.14	15.4														
	IRR		0.1634														

FINANCIAL DECISION-MAKING

The appropriate FX rate for 1993's opening imputed equity is the closing rate for 1992; similarly for the next year. On converting the imputed equities to sterling, their increase is £14.9m, much higher than the difference in dollar terms simply because of the dollar's 10 per cent appreciation between the two years.

As regards 1990, the imputed equity credit is (149.5/2) × 0.1 × (1 − 0.35) = £4.9m. The first term is opening USD imputed equity converted to sterling, the next term is the UK cost of funds, while the last term puts the cost of funds on to a net of UK tax basis. The endowed equity debit and the second tier adjustment are similarly calculated.

Until 1993 the holding gain is zero, as there is no change in FX rates. At the beginning of 1993 the USD appreciates 10 per cent, and in subsequent years its appreciation reflects differential inflation rates. The 1993 holding gain is the opening endowed equity adjusted for the FX movements, i.e. 228.1 [1/1.8182 − 1/2] = £11.4m.

At a 14 per cent COE the NPV is now £15.4m and the IRR 16.3 per cent. The improvement results entirely from the FX movements, showing how important they are, and demonstrating the necessity of attempting to get plausible FX forecasts.

9.9 The Alone Balance Sheet

It is now time to spring an unpleasant surprise. So far all the analysis and discussion have been in terms of the parent's consolidated balance sheet. Some regulators also control the parent's balance sheet; the implications of this fact are shown in Table 9.5.

TABLE 9.5 Consolidated v Alone Balance Sheets (£m)

	Group	Parent	Sub.		Group	Parent	Sub.
Equity	5	5	3	Assets	100	80	20
Second tier	5	5	—	Subsidiary		3	
Capital	10	10	3				
Deposits	90	73	17				
	100	83	20		100	83	20

Using equation 7.4 and assuming second tier capital and deposits cost the same, we find the subsidiary's profits must satisfy the following relation:

International Dimensions

$$SP \geqslant IE(r-i) - EEi$$

In this case:

$$SP \geqslant .05 \times 20(r-i) - 3i$$

that is:

$$SP \geqslant 1(r-i) - 3i$$

In deriving the above relation only the group's capital adequacy was considered. When some regulators, such as the Bank of England, directly consider the parent's capital adequacy, the situation may change. In Chapter 6 it was noted that investments in unconsolidated financial subsidiaries are deducted from capital, which is the approach adopted by the Bank of England when assessing the parent's capital adequacy. When the parent alone is considered, its £3m investment in its subsidiary is an unconsolidated investment. This investment is therefore deducted from the parent's capital of £10m, to get an adjusted figure of £7m for capital adequacy purposes. Provided the capital to RWAs ratio of 10 per cent is maintained, the parent's capital is only sufficient to support assets of £70m – not the £80m it has. As a result, the group balance sheets would have to be those shown in Table 9.6.

TABLE 9.6 Impact of the Alone Balance Sheets (£m)

	Group	Parent	Sub.		Group	Parent	Sub.
Equity	5.0	5.0	3.0	Assets	90.0	70.0	20.0
Second tier	5.0	5.0	–	Subsidiary		3.0	
Capital	10.0	10.0	3.0				
Deposits	80.0	63.0	17.0				
	90.0	73.0	20.0		90.0	73.0	20.0

Before its investment in the subsidiary the parent company and the group had assets of £100m. Therefore as a result of its investment it has had to reduce its own directly held assets by £30m. On the other hand, before its investment its deposits were £90m, so that these have been reduced £27m (that is £90m−£63m). Applying the yield formula 7.2 to the £30m reduction in assets and allowing for the benefit of reduced deposits, we find the parent's investment has cost it:

[103]

$$30[0.05(r-i) + i] - 27i$$

so that, the subsidiary's profits must exceed:

$$1.5(r-i) + 3i$$

This is the same expression as the formula following Table 9.5, except that imputed equity of £1m has been replaced by £1.5m. The equity term is now 50 per cent higher, since the capital to RWAs ratio is 50 per cent higher in the subsidiary.

At a second glance all this may seem unnecessary – surely all that is required is to reduce the subsidiary's equity from £3m to £2m. In the case of a domestic subsidiary this can usually be done, since it will be subject to the same regulatory controls as the parent company, but in the case of a foreign subsidiary the situation is not so simple. Firstly, remitted profits will often be subject to a remittance tax, and, secondly, the local regulator may impose stricter capital adequacy requirements than the parent company's own regulator. In both cases the consequences have to be accepted and allowed for in evaluations.

Sometimes the local regulator's rules will be no stricter than the home regulator's, yet the problem could still arise if limitations are imposed upon the remittance of profits. As far as the parent bank is concerned, it is being forced to maintain a higher level of equity in its subsidiary than a local equivalent. In this case the parental capital constraint may be more severe than the group constraint, and the local capital to RWAs ratio will have to be used. Nevertheless the home regulator will generally allow these forced retentions to count towards the bank's equity base.

In practice there could be a couple of factors mitigating a severe parental constraint. Since the parent company will often have many subsidiaries, it could have surplus capital, and the potential constraint imposed by a particular subsidiary would not come into effect. Moreover, some regulators impose less severe capital adequacy constraints on the parent's than on the consolidated or group balance sheet. If the ratio had been 8.75 per cent instead of 10 per cent in the example used, there would have been no problem.

There is also a different but related problem. In practice markets will quite rightly get nervous about large accumulations of capital in foreign countries, and its view of such forced retentions is likely to be far more demanding than that of regulators. The market itself often provides its own yardstick in the discount it applies to the debt of rescheduling countries. This suggests that the market also applies a discount, perhaps a lesser one, to a bank's capital tied up in such countries. There will be a consequent depression of shareholder value.

10

DEBT SWAPS

10.1 Debt Bond Swaps

Every week, if not every day, the financial press includes items on LDC debt swaps – generally swapping debt for equities, but sometimes existing debt for other hybrid instruments, often partially supported by the government issuing the new instrument. Typical of these latter schemes was the Mexican Bond for Mexican Debt Swap, announced in December 1987.

This scheme offered to swap Mexican public sector debt with a spread of $^{13}/_{16}$ or 0.8125 per cent for a bond with a spread of $1^{5}/_{8}$ per cent, or 1.625 per cent. At maturity the bond's principal was guaranteed by a 20-year zero coupon bond issued by the US Treasury, so there was no risk with regard to final repayment of principal. Of course there was more to it than this. The Mexicans did not envisage exchanging USD1m of nominal debt for USD1m of bonds. Rather for each USD1m of debt they hoped to swap a significantly lesser value of bonds – say USD0.6m or less.

The theory developed in the last two chapters can be used to evaluate these options. The basic framework is not too difficult, but there is considerable detail to work out. First there is a case of 'bygones are bygones' to consider.

10.1.1 Provisions Are Bygones

Once made provisions are bygones. In this context it means that provisions do not have to be funded by deposits and second tier capital. While this may seem a strange, indeed a perverse, proposition, it is easy enough to demonstrate.

To start with, consider a parent company that only has £10bn of assets in its own name. Equity and second tier ratios are 6 per cent and 4 per cent respectively. Its balance sheet is shown in the top half of Table 10.1.

FINANCIAL DECISION-MAKING

TABLE 10.1   Debt Position: before Provisioning (£m)

	Group	Parent	DG[1]		Group	Parent	DG[1]
Equity	600	600	–	Assets	10000	10000	–
Second tier	400	400	–				
Total capital	1000	1000	–				
Deposits	9000	9000	–				
	10000	10000	–		10000	10000	–

Debt Position: after Provisioning (£m)

	Group	Parent	DG[1]		Group	Parent	DG[1]
Equity	642	642	–	Assets	10700	10000	700
Second tier	428	428	–				
Total capital	1070	1070	–				
Deposits	9630	8930	700				
	10700	10000	700		10700	10000	700

1 DG denotes the Debt Group which holds LDC and similar debt.

Now assume a £1bn investment in LDC debt which has to be immediately written down to £0.7bn. With equity and second tier ratios maintained, the consequent balance sheets are shown in the second half of the table.

The equity cost of this investment consists of the £0.3bn write-off which has to be immediately offset against shareholders' funds, plus the £0.42bn needed to support the LDC debt's written-down value of £0.7bn. In addition the bank has increased its second tier capital by £0.028bn, which is 4 per cent of the debt's written-down value. Finally group deposits have increased £0.63bn, comprising the £0.70bn shown in the Debt Group's balance sheet less the £0.07bn reduction in the parent company's debt. Bringing all this together, the original £1bn of debt is financed as follows:

	£bn
Equity write off	0.300
Equity to support book value of LDC debt	0.042
Additional tier 2 capital	0.028
Addition deposit	0.630
	1.000

Debt Swaps

In fact only £0.658bn of deposits and second tier capital are needed to support the LDC debt. The balance of £0.042bn, to bring the 'funding' to £0.7bn, is provided by the £0.042bn of imputed equity needed to support the debt's book value.

It is important to note that the equity write-off of £300m is not entirely borne by the bank's shareholders. A proportion, depending upon the generosity of the authorities, will be born by taxpayers, and in some countries all such provisions can be set against profits for tax purposes.

Shareholders might not be prepared to provide the required equity of £342m. In that case the only course open to the bank is to reduce its non-LDC assets until the equity and capital ratios are at the required levels. It is left as an exercise for the reader to show that the same results obtain if the capital ratios remain unchanged.

Once the provision has been made, the new equity injected and/or other assets run down, the £300m write-off becomes a bygone – it is history. As such, the future cashflows will be the income generated by the LDC assets less the funding costs of the £630m of deposits and £28m of second tier capital. However, the equity of £42m needed to support the written-down value of the LDC assets is still relevant. It has to be compared with the equity needed to support any alternative option – in this case the bond issued by the Mexicans.

10.1.2 New Monies

Under the rescheduling agreements between debtor countries and the banks the latter have to provide additional loans or new monies. They are taken as a percentage of the nominal value of the debtor's current outstandings. New monies have been significant, and have enabled the indebted countries to carry on paying interest on previous outstandings, which has advantages for the banks. Since interest is formally paid on time, banks are not forced to make even larger provisions, and they can, in the short term at least, maintain their equity.

Nevertheless new monies have their own problems. Under most countries' regulations provisions have to be made against new monies at the same rate as those on existing outstandings. The options under consideration are the retention of existing debt or swapping some of it for a bond. Thus provisions against future new monies are real costs, since they would not occur if the swap is made. The same applies to the equity needed to support the written-down value of the future new monies.

10.1.3 *Additional Provisions*

Many observers feel that current provisioning levels against problem country debts are inadequate in many countries. Certainly the need for new monies gives some credence to this view, quite apart from the appalling economic conditions many of these countries still experience. The timing and level of additional provisions, however, are matters for conjecture.

Extra provisions have two effects: firstly, they are deductions from the equity flows, offset by any tax relief, and, secondly, the level of imputed equity is reduced in line with the provisions. Obviously the first impact is far greater than the second. In the case of the bond, final payment is not in doubt, so no provisions against principal are required.

10.1.4 *Expected Values*

Provisions are required, since there is doubt about the repayment of principal and interest. The market's expectation can be directly estimated by taking the ratio of USD interest rates to the interest rate that discounts the annual yield on debt back to its market value. But as long as new monies put off the day of reckoning, it could be argued that interest will continue to be repaid.

While there is no doubt about the repayment of bond's principal at the end of 20 years, the same is not necessarily true of the interest which is paid by the Mexican authorities. The Mexicans, and their agents, tried to give the impression that there was a greater likelihood of interest being paid on the bond than on the debt, though there was absolutely no legal foundation for this view. Nevertheless it was argued that the Mexicans had always been punctilious in paying interest on bonds and that this was reflected in the price of other Mexican government bonds. Again it is very much a matter of judgement whether such arguments are accepted. Debt-forgiveness is often talked about. If it did happen, it would only apply to the debt and not the bond. The model allows debt-forgiveness to be factored in, and a sensitivity analysis is undertaken. A more rigorous approach to probabilities is discussed in Section 10.5.

10.2 The Model: Existing Debt

Table 10.2 shows how the NPV of retaining existing debt is calculated. The first half of the table is specified in USD, the currency of the debt. In

Debt Swaps

TABLE 10.2 NPV of Existing Debt

		Year 1	2	3	4	5	17	18	19	20
1	Additional debt provision	0.00	0.00	0.00	0.00	0.15	0.00	0.00	0.00	0.00
2	Cumulative debt provision		0.35	0.35	0.35	0.35	0.50	0.50	0.50	0.50	0.50
3	Nominal value debt		100.00	105.00	110.25	115.76	121.55	218.29	229.20	240.66	252.70
4	Book value debt		65.00	68.25	71.66	75.25	60.78	109.14	114.60	120.33	126.35
5	Imputed equity		3.90	4.10	4.30	4.51	3.65	6.55	6.88	7.22	7.58
6	Endowed equity		0.00	0.00	0.00	0.00	0.00	0.00	0.00	0.00	0.00
	PROFIT AND LOSS ACCOUNT: DEBT										
7	Expected value yield		8.81	9.25	9.72	10.20	10.71	19.24	20.20	21.21	22.27
8	Expected value deposit		(5.20)	(5.46)	(5.73)	(6.02)	(4.86)	(8.73)	(9.17)	(9.63)	(10.11)
9	PBT		3.61	3.79	3.98	4.18	5.85	10.51	11.03	11.58	12.16
10	Tax		(1.26)	(1.33)	(1.39)	(1.46)	(2.05)	(3.68)	(3.86)	(4.05)	(4.26)
11	PAT		2.35	2.47	2.59	2.72	3.80	6.83	7.17	7.53	7.90
12	FX Rate	1.00	1.00	1.00	1.00	1.00	1.00	1.00	1.00	1.00
13	Yearly FX impact on provisions		0.00	0.00	0.00	0.00	0.00	0.00	0.00	0.00	0.00
14	Sterling equity	3.90	4.10	4.30	4.51	3.65	3.83	6.88	7.22	7.58	0.00
	STERLING EQUITY FLOWS: GBP										
15	PAT	(3.90)	2.35	2.47	2.59	2.72	3.80	6.83	7.17	7.53	7.90
16	Imputed equity		(0.19)	(0.20)	(0.21)	0.87	(0.18)	(0.33)	(0.34)	(0.36)	7.58
17	Imputed equity int.		0.20	0.21	0.22	0.23	0.19	0.34	0.36	0.38	0.39
18	Pre tax WO new money		(1.75)	(1.84)	(1.93)	(2.89)	(3.04)	(5.46)	(5.73)	(6.02)	(6.32)
19	Tax credit on WO		0.61	0.64	0.68	1.01	1.06	1.91	2.01	2.11	2.21
20	Additional write-offs (BT)		0.00	0.00	0.00	(17.36)	0.00	0.00	0.00	0.00	0.00
21	Tax cr. add WO		0.00	0.00	0.00	6.08	0.00	0.00	0.00	0.00	0.00
22	Pre-tax terminal debt loss										0.00
23	Tax cr. term debt loss		0.00	0.00	0.00	0.00	0.00	0.00	0.00	0.00	0.00
24	FX impact on prov.,s	0.00	0.00	0.00	0.00	0.00	0.00	0.00	0.00	0.00	0.00
25	Equity flows	(3.90)	1.22	1.28	1.34	(9.35)	1.83	3.29	3.46	3.63	11.77
	NPV at 0.14	2.57									

FINANCIAL DECISION-MAKING

the second half sterling, the currency in which the equity flows are normally calculated, can be used.

The rate at which provisions are made is shown in rows 1 and 2. Row 2 shows the cumulative opening provision rate, while row 1 gives the annual increases in the provisioning rate. The debt's nominal value is shown in row 3; it grows at 5 per cent p.a. to reflect the anticipated incidence of new monies. At the beginning of year 2 the book value of the debt is USD68.25m (row 4), obtained by reducing the USD105m of nominal debt by the 35 per cent provision shown in row 2. Imputed equity is 6 per cent of the debt's written-down value, while the Debt Group's endowed equity is zero. The differential cost of debt compared to deposits is ignored, since it is not material in this context.

The profit and loss account imposes new complications. USD LIBOR is taken to be 8 per cent; as the spread is 0.8125 per cent, the yield on the debt's nominal value is 8.8125 per cent. Thus in year 5 earnings are $121.55 \times 0.088125 = $ USD10.7m. In its own accounts the Debt Group pays interest on the book value of the debt, so that year 4's interest is $75.25 \times 0.08 = $ USD6.02m. Note that the interest credit on imputed equity is given in row 16. Profits before tax (row 9) are taxed at an appropriate rate, here 35 per cent, to give profits after tax (row 11).

In this example FX rates (row 12) have been kept constant to facilitate the explanation of the items making up the equity flows. Profits after tax are simply taken from row 11. Imputed equity is calculated in the normal way, as is the imputed equity credit (rows 14 and 17 respectively).

At the end of year 1 the nominal value of the debt increases to USD105m as a result of new monies. On provisioning at a rate of 35 per cent against the new monies of USD5m, a USD1.75m provision is created; this is a deduction from the bank's equity (row 18). At 35 per cent the tax relief on this is USD0.61m (row 19). In practice the authorities may not allow all the provision to be offset against profits. If so, the tax credit will have to be amended accordingly.

For purely illustrative purposes, the provisioning rate at the beginning of year 5, or at the end of year 4, is increased to 50 per cent. From this time on, the debt's book value is only 50 per cent of its nominal value. As a result of the increased provisioning rate, 15 per cent has to be written off all previous outstandings of USD115.76m. The write-off amounts to USD17.37m, and is shown in row 20. Tax relief at 35 per cent is shown in the next row.

At the end of year 20 it is assumed that the debt can be sold for its book value. Hence there is no gain or loss. However, row 22 allows for any such gain or loss to be incorporated for those courageous enough to take a view. The next row allows the tax consequences to be factored into the

Debt Swaps

calculations. Alternatively, the evaluation could be done in perpetuity on the assumption that interest, but not principal, will be paid.

Although exchange rates have been held constant for expository purposes, FX movements will affect the sterling levels of provisions, and hence equity levels. Suppose that between the beginning of years 1 and 2 the dollar appreciates 10 per cent, i.e. it goes from USD1 = £1 to USD [1.0/1.1]. The absolute level of sterling imputed equity will be correct, but year 1's opening provision will increase from £35m to £38.5m. This increase will have to be written off against the bank's existing equity, and be replaced by an infusion of new equity, which is shown in row 13. These additional equity requirements are deducted, net of tax relief, from the equity flows in row 24.

Returning to the initial assumption of constant FX rates, we find the net equity flows are shown in row 25. When discounted at 14 per cent, their NPV is £2.57m. Whether or not retaining debt is worthwhile depends upon the NPV of bonds. This calculation is shown in Table 10.3.

10.2.1 Bond Valuation

Compared to the debt model, valuing bonds is straightforward. The bank makes an offer for bonds at, say, a 35 per cent discount on the debt's nominal value. If this is acceptable to the Mexicans, the bond would have a nominal and book value of USD65m (rows 1 and 2). No new monies are required, so its value remains at USD65m throughout the 20 years. Imputed equity is again 6 per cent of book value, and the endowed equity of the Debt Group zero.

In the profit and loss account the expected yield on the bond is LIBOR at 8 per cent, plus a spread of 1.625 per cent, so that income is USD6.26m every year. Since the Debt Group has no endowed equity, its deposits are also USD65m, and at 8 per cent these cost USD5.2m. Pre- and post-tax profits are calculated accordingly (rows 7 and 9).

No FX rates are shown, as these are picked up from the debt section of the model.

The first row of the equity flows shows the USD profits after tax, which can be converted to sterling. Initial imputed equity is 6 per cent of USD65m; since the book value of the bond remains unchanged, there are no further increments of equity. Imputed equity interest is calculated in the normal way.

Had the book value of the bond exceeded that of the debt, it might, under some regulatory regimes, have been possible to reduce provisions accordingly. Equity would be correspondingly boosted and would be a

TABLE 10.3 NPV of Swapping into Bonds

			Year 1	2	3	4	5	18	19	20
1	Nominal value bond		65.00	65.00	65.00	65.00	65.00	65.00	65.00	65.00
2	Book value bond		65.00	65.00	65.00	65.00	65.00	65.00	65.00	65.00
3	Imputed equity		3.90	3.90	3.90	3.90	3.90	3.90	3.90	3.90
4	Endowed equity		0.00	0.00	0.00	0.00	0.00	0.00	0.00	0.00
	PROFIT AND LOSS ACCOUNT: DEBT									
5	Expected value yield		6.26	6.26	6.26	6.26	6.26	6.26	6.26	6.26
6	Expected value deposit		(5.20)	(5.20)	(5.20)	(5.20)	(5.20)	(5.20)	(5.20)	(5.20)
7	PBT		1.06	1.06	1.06	1.06	1.06	1.06	1.06	1.06
8	Tax		(0.37)	(0.37)	(0.37)	(0.37)	(0.37)	(0.37)	(0.37)	(0.37)
9	PAT		0.69	0.69	0.69	0.69	0.69	0.69	0.69	0.69
	STERLING EQUITY FLOWS: GBP									
10	PAT		0.69	0.69	0.69	0.69	0.69	0.69	0.69	0.69
11	Imputed equity	(3.90)	0.00	0.00	0.00	0.00	0.00	0.00	0.00	3.90
12	Imputed equity int.		0.20	0.20	0.20	0.20	0.20	0.20	0.20	0.20
13	Pre tax loss/gain on bond		0.00							
14	Tax on loss/gain		0.00							
15	Tax cr. original WO		0.00							
	NCFs	(3.90)	0.89	0.89	0.89	0.89	0.89	0.89	0.89	4.79
	NPV at 0.14	1.99								

gain to this option. However, if the swap rate is 60 per cent, the bond's book value would be USD60m, and an additional write-off of USD5m would be required. This extra equity cost (or gain in the previous example) is shown in row 13. If the authorities allow any of this extra write-off for tax purposes, the appropriate tax credit is shown in row 14.

At the time of this particular deal the British authorities would not allow any write-back of provisions, though they did require extra provisions if the bond's book value was less than the debt's. It was assumed that any extra provisions could be offset against profits for tax purposes, at least on a deferred basis. If tax is written back into profits on a deferred basis, then strictly the cost of funding the implied equity payment to shareholders should be deducted from the equity flows.

10.3 Comparative Economics

With the illustrative assumptions used, but with provisions at 35 per cent throughout, retaining debt shows an NPV of USD6.8m. Bonds, how-

Debt Swaps

ever, only show a NPV of USD1.99m, to give a difference of USD4.81m in favour of debt.

However, the assumptions used were not necessarily realistic. The sensitivity of the results to various assumptions is shown in Table 10.4. On this basis a view can be taken on whether or not it is worth swapping debt for bonds.

TABLE 10.4 Sensitivity Analysis: NPV USD (Debt–Bonds) M

Swap rate (%)	0.0%	3.5%	5.0%	7.5%
		New monies Increase p.a.		
100	8.6	5.6	3.6	(0.3)
90	8.9	5.9	4.1	–
80	9.2	6.2	4.4	0.3
75	9.3	6.3	4.5	0.5
70	9.5	6.5	4.7	0.6
65	9.7	6.6	4.8	0.8
60	12.3	9.3	7.5	3.4

Assumptions: initial provisions 35 per cent, no further provisions, USD evaluation.

The top row shows various annual percentage increases in new monies, while the first column shows the rate at which the opening nominal value of debt is swapped for bonds. The general drift of the results is not surprising. New monies have a significant deleterious impact; as soon as they are lent, 35 per cent of their value has to be written off. Even after a tax credit this has a large negative impact on the equity flows.

An increasingly adverse swap rate has a comparatively small impact, because the bonds are not especially attractive in their own right, giving a relatively low return on imputed equity. Moreover, when the initial book value of the bonds exceeds that of the debt, no write-back of the difference was allowed in the UK. But when the swap rate falls below 65 per cent, additional provisions are required; hence the large movement in favour of debt at the 60 per cent swap rate.

On the basis of past experience new monies of around 5 per cent p.a. could be regarded as a reasonable guess. Even so, there is still a significant advantage to debt. At a 100 per cent swap rate it is USD3.6m per USD100m of nominal debt. Assuming that the Mexicans were looking for a swap ratio no higher than 60 per cent to 65 per cent, new monies would have to grow at well over 7.5 per cent p.a. to make swapping worthwhile. This is unlikely.

Significant increases in new monies are no doubt consistent with a near certainty of receiving interest payments. Nevertheless they are hardly consistent with maintaining present book values of debt. It could well be argued that an annual 5 per cent increase in new monies really means that the value of the asset is also declining at the same rate. Even if this argument is regarded as facile, it seems far more likely that the provisioning rate will have to increase, rather than remain static.

Table 10.5 shows the impact of a once and for all increase in the provisioning rate 5 years hence. The differing provision levels are also combined with various debt-forgiveness assumptions.

TABLE 10.5 Sensitivity Analysis: NPV (Debt–Bonds)

Percentage of debt-forgiveness	\multicolumn{5}{c}{Additional provisioning rate 5 years hence}
	0%	5%	10%	15%	20%
0	4.8	3.4	2.0	0.6	(0.8)
5	2.6	1.2	(0.3)	(1.7)	(3.1)
10	0.3	(1.1)	(2.5)	(3.9)	(5.3)
20	(4.2)	(5.6)	(7.0)	(8.4)	(9.8)

Assumptions: swap ratio 65 per cent, new monies growing at 5 per cent p.a., USD evaluation.

When no debt-forgiveness is assumed, provisions of around 17 per cent, 5 years hence, tip the evaluation in favour of bonds. Extra provisions of this magnitude could be judged as very likely within the next few years. If there is a slight possibility of debt-forgiveness, then the balance begins to move more strongly in favour of bonds, provided the swap ratio is no worse than 65 per cent. However, with very high levels of debt-forgiveness new monies are unlikely to be required.

Quite clearly the analysis gives no ultimate answer, but it does show what the key assumptions are, and what values have to be placed on them to tip a decision one way or another. Nevertheless, if debt forgiveness is thought likely, the decision starts to swing towards bonds.

10.4 Debt Equity Swaps

With all that has gone before, the technical aspects of swapping into equities are already known. The outlines of the methodology are shown

Debt Swaps

in Table 10.6. The basic options are similar to those in the debt bond swap case, except here Brazilian debt, say, is swapped for Brazilian equities.

With a debt/equity swap rate of 80 per cent, USD80.0m of Brazilian equities can be bought for every USD100.0m of nominal debt. Row 1 shows the latter, while row 4 shows the former. Under UK regulations a provision has to be made against the USD80m of equities, though this is not always the case under other jurisdictions. By applying the same 35 per cent provision that applies to Brazilian debt to the nominal value of the equities, their book value becomes USD52m (row 5). Thus an additional provision of USD13m has to be made, this being the book value of debt less the book value of the equities. The extra provisions are a depletion of the bank's equity and must be deducted from the equity flows (row 14). Under the UK tax regime the extra provision cannot be set against profits, and consequently row 15 shows a zero tax credit.

In this example a constant dividend of 8 per cent on the equities' nominal value has been assumed, to give dividend income of USD6.4m,

TABLE 10.6 NPV of Swapping into Equities

			Year 1	2	3	4	5	10	11	12
1	Nominal value of debt		100.00							
2	Net book value debt		65.00							
3	Discount on nominal debt value		0.20							
4	Nominal value of equity		80.00							
5	Book value of equity		52.00							
6	Dividend rate		0.08							
7	Dividend growth		1.00							
	PROFIT AND LOSS ACCOUNT									
8	Dividend income			6.40	6.40	6.40	6.40	6.40	6.40	6.40
9	Cost of finance			(4.16)	(4.16)	(4.16)	(4.16)	(4.16)	(4.16)	(4.16)
10	PBT			2.24	2.24	2.24	2.24	2.24	2.24	2.24
11	Tax			(0.78)	(0.78)	(0.78)	(0.78)	(0.78)	(0.78)	(0.78)
12	PAT			1.46	1.46	1.46	1.46	1.46	1.46	1.46
	EQUITY FLOWS									
13	Imputed equity	(3.12)								3.12
14	Extra provision	(13.00)								28.00
15	Tax credit	0.00								0.00
16	PAT			1.46	1.46	1.46	1.46	1.46	1.46	1.46
17	IE credit			0.16	0.16	0.16	0.16	0.16	0.16	0.16
18	CGT									0.00
		(16.12)		1.62	1.62	1.62	1.62	1.62	1.62	32.74
	NPV at 0.14	(0.44)								

as shown in row 8. The cost of funding is 8 per cent of USD52m, or USD4.16m, which is shown in row 9. Profits before and after tax are shown in the normal way, and the post-tax profit is shown in row 16 of the equity flows. The imputed equity credit is calculated in the normal manner.

Current Brazilian regulations formally allow the equities to be sold and the proceeds remitted after 12 years. If they are sold at cost, which was USD80m, then there is a net gain of USD28m on their book value. This gain fully enhances the bank's equity, and is added to the equity flows at the end of year 12. Had the equities been increasing in value, they would be subject to a dealing gains tax on sale. In the UK the difference between the purchase and sale price, whether positive or negative, is taxed at 35 per cent. However, if the swap had been used to purchase a stake in a foreign enterprise, the tax implication on sale would be different. Moreover, any USD funds remitted in excess of the purchase price would be subject to a remittance tax, assuming currency was available.

If there are no terminal tax payments and sale is for USD80m, the NPV is minus USD0.44m, though even this result required some pretty heroic assumptions. It is assumed that at the end of the 12 years the equities can be sold, and their price converted to USD and repatriated to the UK. Given the problems of the rescheduling countries, this must be questionable. It would probably be more realistic to assume an income stream in perpetuity, which would give rise to a negative NPV of USD4.6m. Dividend growth mitigates the picture. With dividends growing at 3 per cent p.a. discounting profits only over 25 years gives a NPV of minus USD2.47m.

Debt equity swaps do not appear to have much going for them, at least not in a UK context, unless significant debt-forgiveness is assumed, in which case the comparative economics are transformed.

10.5 An Alternative Approach Applied to Debt Property Swaps

10.5.1 General Considerations

Shareholder value is concerned with maximising a bank's market capitalisation. This standpoint suggests that a direct assessment of the market's valuation of debt, on the one hand, and a swap into, say, property, on the other, should be the evaluation criterion applied. Thus the market might give an equal value to Brazilian debt held by the central

Debt Swaps

bank and to an investment in Brazilian property. If so, and other considerations being equal, then banks too should be indifferent between the two investments. Only if the market clearly prefers one option to the other should the banks opt for it.

10.5.2 The Swap

Under Brazilian regulations some debt can be swapped at par, or nominal, value, for property or other investments in Brazil. Alternatively, it can be left with the central bank, where it will attract no new monies. The question is whether to leave the money on deposit with the central bank or swap into property.

10.5.3 Valuing Debt: a Probability Interpretation

A market for rescheduling debt exists. Provided stockmarkets accept this value, the value of the debt retention option is given. However, no market exists, outside Brazil, for property investment companies with a solely Brazilian portfolio. It is possible nevertheless to use the information provided by the market value of debt to make an estimate of the property company's hypothetical value.

As a first approximation, it seems reasonable to regard investments in debt being undertaken in perpetuity. For example, Brazilian debt may stand at a 60 per cent discount on its nominal value, while its nominal yield is 9 per cent. With these assumptions a USD40m investment in such debt would yield USD9m, to give a return of 9.00/40 or 22.5 per cent. One may assume that a nominal USD bond would also yield 9 per cent.

A comparison of the 22.5 per cent and the 9 per cent can be given an interpretation in terms of probabilities. Assume the 9 per cent return is more or less certain, or at least take it as a base for comparison. In effect the market is saying that the initial probability of receiving debt interest is only 1.09/1.225 or 0.89. In the following year the probability is 0.89^2, in the year after that 0.89^3 and so on. Alternatively, it can be stated that the market assesses the probability of default at 11 per cent.

This interpretation can be confirmed by noting:

$$\frac{22.5 \times 0.89}{(1.09)} + \frac{22.5 \times 0.89^2}{(1.09)^2} + \ldots + \ldots$$

equals:

$$\frac{22.5}{(1.09)} \times [1.09/1.225] + \frac{22.5}{(1.09)^2} [1.09/1.225]^2 + \ldots + \ldots$$

equals:

$$\frac{22.5}{(1.225)} + \frac{22.5}{(1.225)^2} + \ldots + \ldots$$

which is USD100m, since it is an investment yielding 22.5 per cent in perpetuity, discounted at 22.5 per cent.

If banks purchased debt in the secondary market, they might judge that they would have to provide new monies. If so, only 9 per cent would be earned on the new monies, though tax relief might be available on any provisions that had to be made. If new monies are factored into the calculations, then the implied default probability can fall to around half the 11 per cent estimated above.

10.5.4 Valuing Property

It could be assumed that the probability of dividend remittances is the same as interest payments from the central bank. But first it is necessary to value a property investment in the absence of cross-border or remittance risk.

The following assumptions are made about the hypothetical property investment company:

- USD profits of 9m annually pre-tax
- Brazilian tax 63.7 per cent
- all profits remitted
- COE 15 per cent
- cost of borrowings, net of tax, 5.8 per cent
- equity funding 10 per cent and debt funding 90 per cent
- therefore weighted cost of capital 6.765 per cent.

With these assumptions the investment yields USD3.267m p.a., net of Brazilian tax. Discounting this income stream in perpetuity at 6.765 per cent gives a present value of 3.267/0.06765, or USD48.3m. Thus, even if the remittance risk is ignored, the 'discount' on a USD100m property investment is over 50 per cent, mainly due to the onerous rate of taxation. When the probability of non-remittance is factored in, the present value becomes:

$$\frac{3.267}{(1.06765)} \times [0.89] + \frac{3.267}{(1.06765)^2} \times [0.892]^2 + \ldots + \ldots$$

that is:

$$\frac{3.267}{(1.20)} + \frac{3.267}{(1.20)^2} + \ldots + \ldots$$

which is 3.267/0.20 and which equals USD16.3m.

Thus if the probability of repayment is the same in both cases, property has well under half the debt's market value. It is also possible to calculate the break-even probability factor from the relationship $3.267/r = 40$, where r is the discount rate and equals 8.1675 per cent. Comparison with the original 6.765 per cent cost of capital shows a probability of profit remittance being 0.987 (i.e. 1.06765/1.081675). Hence shareholders would only be indifferent between debt and property if the probability of profit remittance is 9.7 per cent better than interest payments by the central bank.

10.5.5 Taxation

Debt swaps usually have tax implications. This case gave the option of investing in the property through a wholly owned Brazilian subsidiary. Under Bank of England rules this means any provision against the original debt can be released. Consequently the tax authorities will claw back the tax credit they allowed when the provision was made, which will be a cost to the swap, and will almost certainly require future provisioning against the debt. This will not affect its current market value, but the future tax relief that goes with the provision will be worth something. These considerations, though not quantified here, further push the decision in favour of retaining the debt.

10.6 Debt-forgiveness

This is a topic which is anathema to the world of finance, but which always lurks in the background. It was briefly mentioned in previous sections to this chapter and its implications alluded to. Conceptually the market price of debt will reflect the market's current assessment of debt-forgiveness, but large scale debt-forgiveness has major implications.

Major forgiveness, say 50 per cent plus, might enable rescheduling countries to service their remaining obligations. If so, the probability of additional default on all remaining obligations becomes minimal, or at least much reduced. Thus the discount factor to be applied when estimating the market value of equities, or other swap options, would not be much higher than that applied to similar investments in the UK.

11

THE INTEGRATED MODEL

11.1 Basic Structure

No model can hope to cope with all circumstances and problems. The model developed in this chapter is designed to cope with the evaluation of business strategies and similar types of evaluations. In Chapter 7 a practical example of the banking model was given, but most of the key input was produced exogenously to the model. The integrated model pulls together the production of all the input needed to evaluate a business or strategy, and provides a useful resumé of many of the areas covered.

Its basic structure consists of various inputs that are initially used to calculate both profits and imputed equity. These are then converted to equity flows, and the DCF analysis undertaken. To start with various environmental assumptions are built into the model. These consist of tax rates, long-term growth rates, the yields on assets and the costs of various types of deposits.

Next the asset side of the balance sheet is forecast and entered; likewise for contingents. All these items are specifically forecast for, say, 5 to 10 years. Thereafter a view is taken on their annual growth rates. In like vein the liabilities side of the balance sheet is forecast. Special emphasis must be given to forecasting levels of the cheaper sources of deposits. The balance sheet automatically balances by adjusting borrowings from the money market.

All these sets of information are combined to produce net interest income and imputed equity. Non-funds-based income is forecast to complete the total income picture. Specific forecasts of various categories of costs are made for 5 to 10 years ahead; costs can then be individually escalated at assumed long-run rates. The profit and loss account is then produced. Once foreign exchange rates have been forecast, sufficient information is available to undertake the financial evaluation.

Usually all balance sheet figures, costs and other items are forecast to

FINANCIAL DECISION-MAKING

grow at the same rate, once explicit forecasts are no longer made. This rate is usually the economy's estimated long-run real growth rate, upped for the inflation factor built into the COE. There are three sets of assumptions implicit in this approach. Firstly, that balance sheet growth, with continuing investment in technology is sufficient to restrict unit wage costs to the general rate of inflation; secondly, that financial activity grows in line with the economy; and finally that market shares are maintained.

The rest of this chapter examines the model's structure in some detail. It should be quite sufficient to enable anyone to produce their own model with at most two days' work on a PC.

11.2 Environmental Assumptions

This example relates to a foreign operation, and Table 11.1 displays the environmental assumptions. Detailed forecasts have been made for the first 6 years. Thereafter the foreign economy's real economic, or GDP, growth has been forecast at 3 per cent p.a., while its inflation has been forecast at 5 per cent p.a. Combined, these give nominal growth of 8.15 per cent. All forecast items have been increased at this rate from year 7 onwards.

Local corporation tax is 25 per cent, compared with UK tax of 35 per cent. Remitted profits, which are often subject to taxation, are based on profits after local taxation. When the UK rate exceeds the local rate, additional tax is levied by the UK Revenue to make up the difference. These calculations are shown in Table 11.4 (rows 275 to 280). UK and local inflation rates are used to determine exchange-rate movements 6 years out; they are the same, and therefore consistent with the cost of funds being 10 per cent in both countries from year 6 onwards.

The imputed equity ratio shown is 7 per cent, which assumes a 10 per cent capital ratio, general provisions at 1 per cent of RWA, and a subordinated debt ratio of 3 per cent. The latter costs 0.5 per cent more than the UK costs of funds. Financial trade investments have a 67 per cent equity weighting, since it is assumed that no general provisions are required.

The next set of data in Table 11.1 shows the local cost of funds and the margins earned on assets. Assets are classified by the five categories of risk weights. All assets are assumed to earn the local cost of funds plus a margin. Cash, however, yields no income, and to reflect this its margin must exactly offset the cost of funds. For example, in year 6 the local cost of funds is 10 per cent and the margin on cash is minus 10 per cent – similarly for other assets that yield less than the cost of funds.

The Integrated Model

TABLE 11.1 The Integrated Model: Environmental Assumptions

6	APPRAISAL OF INTERNATIONAL PROJECTS:						
7							
8	04-Jan-89						
9	11:44 AM						
10							
11	ENVIRONMENTAL ASSUMPTIONS						
12							
13	GDP Growth	3.00%	Local tax	25.00%			
14	Inflation	5.00%	UK tax	35.00%			
15	Asset growth	8.15%					
16	Revenue growth	8.15%	UK inflation	5.00%			
17	Costs growth:		Domestic inflation	5.00%			
18	1 Staff	8.15%	Remittance tax	10.00%			
19	2 Prem. & equipment	8.15%	Debt ratio	3.00%			
20	3 Other	8.15%	Addit. cost of debt	0.50%			
21	4	8.15%	Trade investments	67.00%			
22	5 CM/HO costs	8.15%	Imputed equity ratio	7.00%			
25	MARGINS OVER LOCAL COST OF FUNDS						
26							
27		Year 1	2	3	4	5	6
28							
29	Local cost of funds	14.600%	12.500%	12.000%	11.300%	10.700%	10.000%
30							
31	Margin on RWA at 0%						
32	Cash – general	−14.600%	−12.500%	−12.000%	−11.300%	−10.700%	−10.000%
33	Cash – reserve requirement	−14.600%	−12.500%	−12.000%	−11.300%	−10.700%	−11.000%
34	Group balances	−10.120%	−7.415%	−7.000%	−6.300%	−5.700%	−6.000%
35		0.000%	0.000%	0.000%	0.000%	0.000%	0.000%
36	Margin on RWA at 10%						
37	Treasury bills	−10.180%	0.375%	0.375%	0.375%	0.375%	0.375%
38		0.000%	0.000%	0.000%	0.000%	0.000%	0.000%
39		0.000%	0.000%	0.000%	0.000%	0.000%	0.000%
40		0.000%	0.000%	0.000%	0.000%	0.000%	0.000%
41	Margin on RWA at 20%						
42	Government bonds	2.500%	2.500%	2.500%	2.500%	2.500%	2.500%
43	Statutory investments	1.768%	−0.300%	−0.300%	−0.300%	−0.300%	−0.300%
44	Money mkt assets < 1 year	0.311%	0.000%	0.000%	0.000%	0.000%	0.000%
45	Cheques in course of coll.	−14.600%	−12.500%	−12.000%	−11.300%	−10.700%	−11.000%
46	Margin on RWA at 50%						
47	Mortgage loans	3.000%	3.000%	3.000%	3.000%	3.000%	2.000%
48		0.000%	0.000%	0.000%	0.000%	0.000%	0.000%
49		0.000%	0.000%	0.000%	0.000%	0.000%	0.000%
50		0.000%	0.000%	0.000%	0.000%	0.000%	0.000%
51	Margin on RWA at 100%						
52	Inv. in cos	0.000%	0.000%	0.000%	0.000%	0.000%	0.000%
53	Lending: MNC	1.550%	1.550%	1.410%	1.270%	1.130%	1.000%
54	„ : EP	2.400%	2.400%	2.050%	1.700%	1.350%	1.000%
55	„ : Quoted	3.974%	1.970%	1.920%	1.870%	1.820%	1.750%
56	„ : Middle market	4.083%	2.310%	2.490%	2.670%	2.850%	3.000%
57	Consumer loans	5.000%	5.000%	5.000%	5.000%	5.000%	3.000%
58	Credit cards	7.000%	7.000%	7.000%	7.000%	7.000%	7.000%
59	Other	+3.580%	−11.931%	−11.432%	−10.732%	−10.132%	−10.432%
60	Provisions	−14.600%	−12.500%	−12.000%	−11.300%	−10.700%	−10.000%
61	Premises	−14.600%	−12.500%	−12.000%	−11.300%	−10.700%	−10.000%
64	COST OF DEPOSITS						
65							
66		Year 1	2	3	4	5	6
67							
68	UK cost of funds	10.000%	10.000%	10.000%	10.000%	10.000%	10.000%
69							
70	Local cost of deposits						
71	Sight deposits: Per.	0.000%	2.000%	6.500%	6.500%	6.500%	6.500%
72	„ „ : Cor.	0.000%	3.000%	7.375%	7.375%	7.375%	7.375%
73	Term deposits: Pers.	0.000%	13.125%	12.000%	11.300%	10.700%	9.500%
74	Term deposits: Pers.	14.600%	0.675%	0.675%	0.675%	0.675%	0.675%
75	„ „ : Corp.	14.600%	12.500%	12.000%	11.300%	10.700%	11.000%
76	„ „ : Corp.	14.600%	12.500%	12.000%	11.300%	10.700%	11.000%
77	Current tax	0.000%	0.000%	0.000%	0.000%	0.000%	0.000%
78	Group balances	14.600%	12.500%	12.000%	11.300%	10.700%	11.000%
79	Other	14.600%	12.500%	12.000%	11.300%	10.700%	11.000%
80	FA reval. reserve	0.000%	0.000%	0.000%	0.000%	0.000%	0.000%
81	Money market	14.600%	12.500%	12.000%	11.300%	10.700%	10.000%

FINANCIAL DECISION-MAKING

The final set of imputs shows the costs of various types of deposit. It starts off with the UK cost of funds, which is used for calculating the imputed and endowed equity interest adjustments. The costs of various sources of deposits, consistent with the forecast level of these deposits, are estimated and entered as data. Generally money market rates and the cost of funds will be taken as synonymous, since the former will nearly always be the marginal cost of funds. From year 6 onwards deposit rates and margins are frozen.

11.3 The Balance Sheet and Contingents

Assets, contingent liabilities and liabilities for the first 7 years are shown in Table 11.2. The assets are grouped according to their risk weightings. Explicit forecasts are made for the first 6 years; thereafter all items are grown at 8.15 per cent a year. The weightings shown for contingents are specific to the particular evaluation, and therefore are all inputs to the model.

Not all liabilities are forecast. Local endowed equity, excluding property revaluation reserves, is calculated according to the local rules of the game in relation to the subsidiary's asset structure. All other items apart from current tax and money market liabilities are forecast.

The opening tax figure for year 2 is FF367m. It consists of the local tax charge of FF262m, the additional UK tax of FF105m, plus the remittance tax, which is zero, at the end of year 1. Additional UK taxes are included, since the subsidiary's impact on the consolidated balance sheet is required. Complete accuracy would require the impact to be fed into dummy UK accounts and the consequent effects calculated. Money market funds are the marginal source of deposits, and therefore used as the balancing item. They are taken to be all assets less all other liabilities.

11.4 Net Interest Income

Net interest income, shown in Table 11.3, is derived from the yield on assets less the interest paid on deposits. Yields are calculated from the data given in Tables 11.1 and 11.2. Take the second of the assets risk-weighted at 100 per cent in year 4. Its opening balance sheet value is FF12,366m from Table 11.2; the cost of funds is 11.3 per cent and the appropriate margin 1.27 per cent in year 4. Therefore the asset yields

The Integrated Model

TABLE 11.2 The Integrated Model: Balance Sheet

			Year 1	2	3	4	5	6	7
87	Risk-weighted assets								
88									
89	Weighted at 0%								
90	Cash – general		415	477	545	636	745	805	871
91	Cash – reserve requirement		1,781	2,959	3,752	4,882	6,425	6,949	7,515
92	Group balances		1,793	2,212	2,716	3,461	4,429	5,691	6,155
93			0	0	0	0	0	0	0
94									
95			3,989	5,648	7,013	8,980	11,598	13,445	14,541
96									
97	Weighted at 10%								
98	Treasury bills		1,502	1,637	1,966	2,362	2,837	3,407	3,685
99			0	0	0	0	0	0	0
100			0	0	0	0	0	0	0
101			0	0	0	0	0	0	0
102									
103			1,502	1,637	1,966	2,362	2,837	3,407	3,685
104									
105	Weighted at 20%								
106	Government bonds		0	0	256	590	1,078	1,703	1,842
107	Statutory investments		2,530	1,448	1,713	2,089	2,603	3,307	3,577
108	Money mkt assets < 1 year		3,568	4,101	4,690	5,475	6,405	7,510	8,122
109	Cheques in course of coll.		1,985	2,447	3,004	3,829	4,900	6,297	6,810
110									
111			8,083	7,996	9,663	11,984	14,986	18,817	20,351
112									
113	Weighted at 50%								
114	Mortgage loans		0	0	0	0	0	1,255	1,357
115			0	0	0	0	0	0	0
116			0	0	0	0	0	0	0
117			0	0	0	0	0	0	0
118									
119			0	0	0	0	0	1,255	1,357
120									
121	Weighted at 100%								
122	Inv. in cos		103	0	0	0	0	0	0
123	Lending: MNC		10,013	10,671	11,290	12,366	12,938	13,160	14,233
124	" : EP		5,210	5,212	5,210	5,300	5,175	5,264	5,693
125	" : Quoted		1,329	2,233	3,473	5,300	7,763	10,528	11,386
126	" : Middle market		4,627	6,617	8,862	12,212	17,035	23,393	25,300
127	Consumer loans		0	0	0	0	0	418	452
128	Credit cards		0	0	0	0	0	45	49
129	Other		287	330	377	440	515	604	653
130	Provisions		261	168	224	309	431	592	640
131	Premises		2,454	2,808	3,359	4,019	4,807	5,750	6,219
132	Equipment		508	554	631	719	819	933	1,009
133	Other		272	312	357	417	488	572	619
134									
135			25,064	28,905	33,783	41,081	49,971	61,260	66,252
136									
137	Total Assets		38,638	44,186	52,425	64,406	79,392	98,184	106,186
138									
139	Contingents at	4%	0	0	0	0	0	0	0
140	Contingents at	20%	1,426	2,143	3,137	4,515	6,579	7,115	7,695
141	Contingents at	50%	1,385	2,084	3,050	4,390	6,396	6,918	7,481
142	Contingents at	100%	1,728	2,597	3,801	5,472	7,972	8,622	9,325
143									
144			4,539	6,824	9,988	14,377	20,948	22,655	24,501
145									
146	Liabilities								
147	Endowed equity (local)		3,641	3,823	4,014	4,215	4,426	4,647	4,879
148	Sight deposits: Personal		7,578	10,912	15,268	21,365	29,895	41,832	45,241
149	" " : Corporate		4,751	5,584	6,513	7,950	9,704	11,844	12,809
150	Term deposits: Pers. < 180		1,234	1,234	1,234	1,234	1,234	1,234	1,234
151	Term deposits: Pers. > 180		11,237	11,237	11,237	11,237	11,237	11,237	11,237
152	" " : Corp. < 180		359					0	0
153	" " : Corp. > 180		310					0	0
154	Current tax		461	367	751	664	678	813	745
155	Group balances		31	39	47	60	77	99	108
156	Other		3,905	4,815	5,912	7,534	9,641	12,391	13,401
157	FA reval. reserve		562	852	1,170	1,549	2,004	2,547	2,754
158	Money market		4,569	5,323	6,279	8,598	10,496	11,540	13,777
159									
160			38,638	44,186	52,425	64,406	79,392	98,184	106,186

[125]

FINANCIAL DECISION-MAKING

TABLE 11.3 The Integrated Model: Net Interest Income

		Year 1	2	3	4	5	6	7
162	Revenue account							
163	Gross interest income							
164								
165	Risk-weighted assets at 0%							
166	Cash – general	0	0	0	0	0	0	0
167	Cash – reserve requirement	0	0	0	0	0	0	0
168	Group balances	80	112	136	173	221	228	246
169		0	0	0	0	0	0	0
170								
171		80	112	136	173	221	228	246
172								
173								
174	Risk-weighted assets at 10%							
175	Treasury bills	66	211	243	276	314	353	382
176		0	0	0	0	0	0	0
177		0	0	0	0	0	0	0
178		0	0	0	0	0	0	0
179								
180		66	211	243	276	314	353	382
181								
182								
183	Risk-weighted assets at 20%							
184	Government bonds	0	0	37	81	142	213	230
185	Statutory investments	414	177	200	230	271	321	347
186	Money mkt assets < 1 year	532	513	563	619	685	751	812
187	Cheques in course of coll.	0	0	0	0	0	(63)	(68)
188								
189		946	689	800	930	1,098	1,222	1,321
190								
191								
192	Risk-weighted assets at 50%							
193	Mortgage loans	0	0	0	0	0	151	163
194		0	0	0	0	0	0	0
195		0	0	0	0	0	0	0
196		0	0	0	0	0	0	0
197								
198		0	0	0	0	0	151	163
199								
200								
201	Risk-weighted assets at 100%							
202	Inv. in cos	6	0	0	0	0	0	0
203	Lending: MNC	1,617	1,499	1,514	1,554	1,531	1,448	1,566
204	,, : EP	896	777	732	689	624	579	626
205	,, : Quoted	247	323	483	698	972	1,237	1,338
206	,, : Middle market	864	980	1,284	1,706	2,308	3,041	3,289
207	Consumer loans	0	0	0	0	0	54	59
208	Credit cards	0	0	0	0	0	8	8
209	Other	32	2	2	3	3	(3)	(3)
210	Provisions	0	0	0	0	0	0	0
211	Premises	0	0	0	0	0	0	0
212								
213		3,662	3,581	4,016	4,650	5,437	6,364	6,883
214								
215								
216	Interest income	4,755	4,593	5,195	6,029	7,071	8,318	8,995
217								
218	Interest costs							
219	Sight deposits: Personal	(74)	(218)	(992)	(1,389)	(1,943)	(2,719)	(2,941)
220	,, ,, : Corporate	0	(168)	(480)	(586)	(716)	(873)	(945)
221	Term deposits: Pers. < 180	0	(162)	(148)	(139)	(132)	(117)	(117)
222	Term deposits: Pers. > 180	(1,641)	(76)	(76)	(76)	(76)	(76)	(76)
223	,, ,, : Corp. < 180	(52)	0	0	0	0	0	0
224	,, ,, : Corp. > 180	(45)	0	0	0	0	0	0
225	Current tax	0	0	0	0	0	0	0
226	Group balances	(5)	(5)	(6)	(7)	(8)	(11)	(12)
227	Other	(570)	(602)	(709)	(851)	(1,032)	(1,363)	(1,474)
228	FA reval. reserve	0	0	0	0	0	0	0
229	Money market	(471)	(665)	(754)	(972)	(1,123)	(1,154)	(1,378)
230								
231	Interest expense	(2,858)	(1,896)	(3,165)	(4,020)	(5,030)	(6,314)	(6,942)
232								

The Integrated Model

233 Net interest income	1,897	2,698	2,030	2,009	2,042	2,004	2,053
234							
235 Total RWA (assets)	26,831	30,668	35,912	43,714	53,252	65,991	71,369
236 Total RWA (contingents)	2,706	4,068	5,953	8,570	12,486	13,504	14,604
237 Imputed equity	2,068	2,431	2,931	3,660	4,602	5,565	6,018
238							
239 Endowed equity (Local)	3,641	3,823	4,014	4,215	4,426	4,647	4,879
240							
241 Imputed equity	2,068	2,431	2,931	3,660	4,602	5,565	6,018
242 Trade investment at 67.00%							
243							
244 Total imputed equity	2,068	2,431	2,931	3,660	4,602	5,565	6,018
245							
246 London adjustment	0	0	0	0	0	0	0
247 Local endowed equity	3,641	3,823	4,014	4,215	4,426	4,647	4,879
248							
249 Endowed equity	3,641	3,823	4,014	4,215	4,426	4,647	4,879

12.57 per cent × 12, 366 equals FF1,554m. Deposit costs are similarly obtained. For example, in year 3 money market deposits cost 12 per cent, and they amount to FF6,279, to give a cost of FF754m.

11.5 Profit and Loss Account

Profits are shown in Table 11.4. Income consists of two elements: net interest which was derived in the previous section, and non-funds or fee income. The former is the first item in the profit and loss account. Various sources of non-funds-based income are allowed for; they can be related to the levels of the different types of contingents, or forecast in any way that is appropriate to the circumstances. In this example all types of non-funds-based income have been grouped together, and shown as 'revenue 2'.

Provisions relate to specific provisions only, since general provisions are already incorporated into the imputed equity ratio. Deducting them here would amount to double counting.

Costs are broken out into three categories. Along with all preceding items, they have been forecast for the first 6 years, and then escalated at 8.15 per cent a year.

Profits before tax are initially taxed at the local corporation tax rate. If this is lower than the UK rate, the parent will have to pay the excess to the UK revenue, and the model allows for this. Additionally it is assumed that profits, after local taxation, in excess of those needed to finance the increase in local equity are remitted to the UK. In this example the remittance tax suffered is 10 per cent. Finally earnings net of all taxes are shown.

FINANCIAL DECISION-MAKING

TABLE 11.4 The Integrated Model: Equity Flows

		Year 1	2	3	4	5	6	7
251	Profit and loss account							
252	Income							
253	Revenue 1 net int. inc.	1,897	2,698	2,030	2,009	2,042	2,004	2,053
254	Revenue 2	971	1,038	1,432	1,987	2,775	3,090	3,342
255	Revenue 3	0	0	0	0	0	0	0
256	Revenue 4	0	0	0	0	0	0	0
257								
258	Total inc. before provs	2,868	3,736	3,462	3,996	4,817	5,094	5,395
259								
260	Provisions	(372)	(94)	(128)	(179)	(252)	(351)	(380)
261								
262	Total inc. after provs	2,496	3,642	3,334	3,817	4,565	4,743	5,016
263								
264	Managed costs							
265	1 Staff	(881)	(1,004)	(1,076)	(1,280)	(1,524)	(1,815)	(1,963)
266	2 Prem. and equipment	(219)	(280)	(323)	(395)	(462)	(539)	(583)
267	3 Other	(347)	(386)	(406)	(474)	(554)	(631)	(682)
268	4	0	0	0	0	0	0	0
269								
270	Total managed costs	(1,447)	(1,670)	(1,805)	(2,149)	(2,540)	(2,985)	(3,228)
271	5 CM costs	0	0	0	0	0	0	0
272	6 HO costs	0	0	0	0	0	0	0
273								
274	Total costs	(1,447)	(1,670)	(1,805)	(2,149)	(2,540)	(2,985)	(3,228)
275	Profit before tax	1,049	1,972	1,529	1,668	2,025	1,758	1,787
276	Local tax at 25.00%	(262)	(493)	(382)	(417)	(506)	(439)	(447)
277								
278	Profit after local tax	787	1,479	1,147	1,251	1,518	1,318	1,341
279	Additional UK tax	(105)	(197)	(153)	(167)	(202)	(176)	(179)
280	Tax on rem. prof. at 10.00%	0	(60)	(129)	(95)	(104)	(130)	(109)
281								
282	Currency earnings	682	1,221	865	989	1,212	1,013	1,053
283								
284								
285	FX year end 10.000	11.496	11.605	11.716	11.827	11.827	11.827	11.827
286								
287	FX sensitivities							
288	Local inflation p.a.	1.05						
289	UK inflation p.a.	1.05						
290								
291								
292								
293	Sterling earnings	59.304	105.222	73.831	83.645	102.468	85.647	89.044
294	Imputed equity	(206.756)	(4.754)	(41.012)	(59.865)	(76.685)	(81.417)	(38.345)	(41.470)
295	Imputed equity int.	13.439	13.748	16.414	20.305	25.290	30.582	0.000
296	Endowed equity int.	(23.667)	(21.616)	(22.483)	(23.384)	(24.322)	(25.538)	0.000
297	Tier 2 adjustment	(0.288)	(0.295)	(0.352)	(0.435)	(0.542)	(0.655)	(0.709)
298	Holding gain	(47.378)	(3.137)	(3.263)	(3.393)	0.000	0.000	0.000
299								
300	Net equity flows	(206.756)	(3.343)	52.911	4.282	0.053	21.477	51.691	46.866
301								
302								
303	UK cost of funds	10.00%	10.00%	10.00%	10.00%	10.00%	10.00%	
304	UK tax less 1 65.00%							
305								
306	***							
307	*			*				
308	* NPV at 14.00% ===>	50.463	*					
309	*			*				
310	* IRR: 15.99%			*				
311	*			*				
312	***							
313								
314	Key performance indicators							
315	ROA (pre-tax) %	2.71	4.46	2.92	2.59	2.55	1.79	1.68
316	ROA (post-tax) %	1.76	2.76	1.65	1.54	1.53	1.03	0.99
317	Post-tax ROIE %	24.64	26.89	3.16	1.25	5.66	11.13	9.35
318	Cost/income ratio %	57.98	45.86	54.14	56.31	55.65	62.93	64.36
319	Employees (full time equiv.)							

[128]

The Integrated Model

11.6 Equity

Because of space limitations, risk-weighted assets and imputed equity are shown at the end of Table 11.3. There are no investments in non-consolidated finance companies, so that imputed equity is 7 per cent of risk-weighted assets. The endowed equity figures are replicated for convenience.

So far all figures have been in French francs. FX rates for conversion to sterling are shown half-way down Table 11.4. They are forecast for 5 years, after which they are held constant, reflecting the equality of forecast local and UK inflation rates with local and UK interest rates from year 6 onwards.

Foreign currency earnings net of all taxes are converted to sterling at year-end FX rates and then fed into the equity flow calculation.

Imputed equity is calculated in the normal way, as are the imputed and endowed equity interest adjustments. The adjustment for the extra 0.5 per cent cost of second tier capital is shown. As usual, it only has a negligible impact, amounting to 0.14 per cent of imputed equity. The impact of property revaluations has been ignored. Holding gains are negative for the first 4 years as the French franc depreciates against sterling. Thereafter holding gains are zero.

With all these assumptions the NPV at 14 per cent is £50.5m and the IRR 16 per cent.

It was felt worthwhile spending some time on the integrated model for several reasons. A useful summary of much of the second half of the book is provided. The structure of the model is not complicated, even though there may seem a great deal of detail. In fact it only took a day and a half to produce, using a standard PC language.

Another advantage of the model is that it forces those looking at the business to take a view of, and by implication justify, all key aspects of the business. Nothing is swept under the carpet. All the market assumptions can be compared with recent history, trends, market surveys and analyses, and then judged for plausibility. Cost forecasts too can be rigorously examined. Areas of doubt can be subject to sensitivity analysis. If results are not robust to adverse changes, contingency plans can be drawn, or that aspect of the business run down. The more explicit the assumptions, the more rigorously they can be examined, and weaknesses or undue optimism eliminated. None of this in the end substitutes for good judgement, but that is generally impossible without the work of the model.

12

EVALUATING FIXED ASSET EXPENDITURE

12.1 Back to Basics

Most books on investment appraisal start by giving examples of how to evaluate the benefits of investing in fixed assets, and in a traditional DCF context this is usually the easiest situation to consider. Within banking it is more difficult when premises are considered. This chapter starts off by considering the benefits or costs of purchasing fixed assets other than premises.

12.2 Plant and Equipment: Basic Approach

A decision whether or not to make a £100m investment in fixed assets is required. Table 12.1 sets out the various forecasts available to the decision-makers.

Annual balance sheets are shown in Table 12.1's first section. At the beginning of year 1 fixed assets are shown in the balance sheet at £100m, and at £80m year-end reflecting annual depreciation charges of £20m. By the end of year 5 they will have been completely written off. On the liabilities side second tier capital has been swept into deposits for simplicity of exposition, and the equity ratio taken as 10 per cent. It declines by £2m each year in line with the declining book value of the assets.

In the second section profits are derived from the income generated by the investment. Deduction of depreciation charges (£20m p.a.) and interest (at 10 per cent on deposits) give profits. Equity declines in line with fixed assets, so that incremental equity is negative; this means that it can be paid back to shareholders, or used to support projects elsewhere in the bank. No adjustments have been made for imputed and endowed equity interest, as they have the same values. Equity flows are shown in the final row.

[130]

Evaluating Fixed Asset Expenditure

TABLE 12.1 Accounting Consequences of Fixed Investments (£m)

	Year 1	2	3	4	5
Opening balance sheets					
Fixed assets	100	80	60	40	20
Liabilities					
Equity	10	8	6	4	2
Deposits	90	72	54	36	18
	100	80	60	40	20
Profits year-end					
Income		30.0	28.2	26.4	24.6	22.8
Depreciation		(20.0)	(20.0)	(20.0)	(20.0)	(20.0)
Interest		(9.0)	(7.2)	(5.4)	(3.6)	(1.8)
Profit		1.0	1.0	1.0	1.0	1.0
Imputed equity	(10.0)	2.0	2.0	2.0	2.0	2.0
Equity flow	(10.0)	3.0	3.0	3.0	3.0	3.0
Use of income statement					
Dividend		1.0	1.0	1.0	1.0	1.0
Repayment of equity		2.0	2.0	2.0	2.0	2.0
Interest		9.0	7.2	5.4	3.6	1.8
Deposit repayment		18.0	18.0	18.0	18.0	18.0
		30.0	28.2	26.4	24.6	22.8

Table 12.1's final section is a 'use of income statement', which is similar to the sources and applications of funds statement in Chapter 5. It shows how everything is funded from the project's income. For example, at the end of year 3 dividends of £1m are paid, along with a £2m repayment of equity. Interest payments amount to £5.4m and deposits of £18m are repaid.

12.2.1 The Supporting Balance Sheet

The NPV of the project at 14 per cent is £0.299m, and the IRR is 15.2 per cent, so it appears to be just about worthwhile. Unfortunately only the easy part of the problem has been tackled. Nearly all regulators not only impose capital adequacy constraints but also liquidity requirements, which are generally related to types of deposits. In most circumstances these liquidity constraints amount to saying that certain deposits have to

FINANCIAL DECISION-MAKING

be supported by specified percentages of cash, short-term deposits with banks, government bonds and possibly other liquid assets. It will be assumed that only the first three items apply and that their ratios are 1 per cent, 5 per cent and 20 per cent with respect to total deposits, and that their risk weightings are zero, 20 per cent and 10 per cent respectively. The margins, with respect to the cost of deposits, on government debt and deposits with banks are both taken as 0.25 per cent. With these additional assumptions the new balance sheets and equity flow statements are shown in Table 12.2. It will be left to Chapter 13 to show how such a balance sheet is derived.

Slight differences occur in the annual equity flows, owing to rounding. The NPV and IRR of the resulting equity flows are £0.171m and 14.7 per cent. The introduction of all these complications has hardly made any difference, suggesting that they are hardly worth bothering with. In the

TABLE 12.2 Full Accounting Consequences of Fixed Investments (£m)

	Year 0	1	2	3	4	5
Assets						
Cash		1.21	0.97	0.73	0.48	0.24
Government debt		6.04	4.83	3.63	2.42	1.21
Deposits		24.18	19.34	14.50	9.67	4.84
Fixed assets		100.00	80.00	60.00	40.00	20.00
		131.43	105.14	78.86	52.57	26.29
Liabilities						
Equity		10.54	8.43	6.33	4.22	2.11
Deposits		120.89	96.71	72.53	48.35	24.18
		131.43	105.14	78.86	52.57	26.29
Income						
Revenue		30.00	28.20	26.40	24.60	22.80
Government debt		0.62	0.50	0.37	0.25	0.12
Deposits with banks		2.48	1.98	1.49	0.99	0.50
Total income		33.10	30.68	28.26	25.84	23.42
Depreciation		(20.00)	(20.00)	(20.00)	(20.00)	(20.00)
Interest		(12.09)	(9.67)	(7.25)	(4.83)	(2.42)
Profit		1.01	1.01	1.01	1.01	1.00
IE	(10.54)	2.11	2.10	2.11	2.11	2.11
Equity flows	(10.54)	3.12	3.11	3.12	3.12	3.11

Evaluating Fixed Asset Expenditure

UK this may well be true, but it is certainly not the case in some countries, where liquidity or reserve asset requirements can be very onerous.

For example, in Spain 2.5 per cent of deposits have to be lodged interest-free with the Bank of Spain, with another 17 per cent at a rate of 4 per cent below prevailing money market rates. A further 11 per cent have to be invested in government securities. Even if all these items have a zero risk weighting, the impact on the results is now significant, with the NPV falling to (£0.224m) and the IRR well below 14 per cent at 13.1 per cent. Table 12.3 illustrates the calculations.

Thus, while the derivation of the appropriate balance sheets can be fairly complex, the basic approach itself is straightforward. Unfortunately this is not so when property is considered.

TABLE 12.3 Impact of Liquidity Requirements

	Year 0	1	2	3	4	5
Assets						
Cash (no interest)		3.237	2.590	1.942	1.295	0.647
Cash (interest at 6%)		22.014	17.611	13.208	8.806	4.403
Government bonds		14.245	11.396	8.547	5.697	2.849
Fixed assets		100.000	80.000	60.000	40.000	20.000
		139.496	111.597	83.698	55.798	27.899
Liabilities						
Equity		10.000	8.000	6.000	4.000	2.000
Deposits		129.496	103.597	77.698	51.798	25.899
		139.496	111.597	83.698	55.798	27.899
Income						
Revenue		30.000	28.200	26.400	24.600	22.800
Cash and government bonds		3.717	2.974	2.230	1.487	0.743
Total income		33.717	31.174	28.630	26.087	23.543
Depreciation		(20.000)	(20.000)	(20.000)	(20.000)	(20.000)
Interest		(12.950)	(10.360)	(7.770)	(5.180)	(2.590)
Profit		0.767	0.814	0.860	0.907	0.953
Imputed equity	(10.000)	2.000	2.000	2.000	2.000	2.000
Equity flow	(10.000)	2.767	2.814	2.860	2.907	2.953

NPV = (0.224)
IRR = 13.1 per cent

FINANCIAL DECISION-MAKING

12.3 Investment in Property

Analysing the financial implications of owning property is fairly complex. In the first example a property is bought for £20m, and the costs to the bank explained by means of the group's incremental balance sheets. The illustrative figures are shown in Table 12.4.

TABLE 12.4 Purchase of Property (£m)

	Group	Parent	Sub.		Group	Parent	Sub.
Equity	1.33	1.33	1.60	Assets	20.00	–	20.00
General provisions	–	–	–	Subsidiary		1.60	
Subordinated debt	0.67	0.67	–				
Revaluation reserve	–	–	–				
Total capital	2.00	2.00	1.60				
Deposits	18.00	(0.40)	18.40				
	20.00	1.60	20.00		20.00	1.60	20.00

The only increase in the bank's assets is the £20m cost of the property. It is assumed that the local regulator requires an 8 per cent capital ratio, and that its parent endows it with the required £1.6m. The balance of £18.4m is locally funded by deposits.

Total capital required by the parent to support the property is taken to be 10 per cent, or £2m. However, there will be no general provision against property, nor for the time being will there be any revaluation reserves. Consequently it is assumed that the capital can only consist of equity and subordinated debt, which have to be in the ratio 2:1. All other items in the group balance sheets are derived in the normal way.

Using the normal relationships and symbols, the cost to the parent of the investment is:

$$1.33r + 0.67(i + di) - 0.40i$$

where $1.33r$ is the annual cost of equity, $0.67(i + di)$ the annual cost of subordinated debt, and $0.40i$ the annual savings on reduced parental deposits.

That is:

$$1.33(r-i) + 1.60i + 0.67di$$

[134]

Evaluating Fixed Asset Expenditure

or, on generalising:

$$\text{IE}(r-i) + \text{EE}i + \text{IE}\frac{(\text{SD})}{(\text{IE})}di \quad\quad\quad\quad\quad\quad\quad\quad (12.1)$$

where SD = subordinated debt.

If investment in property is to be worthwhile, the annual benefits must at least equal 12.1. Putting this into a net present value context, as described in Section 7.5, the following NPV must be greater than zero:

$$-\text{IE} + \text{PV(Subsidiary's Profits)} + \text{PV}(\text{IE}i - \text{EE}i - \text{IE}\frac{[\text{SD}]}{[\text{IE}]}di)$$

where the subsidiary's discounted profits are:

PV(Rent Saved) − PV (Cost of deposits)

All this seems straightforward enough and breaks no new ground. Note, however, that no attempt has been made to create a supporting balance sheet. Whether or not this sophistication is necessary depends upon the stringency of local liquidity requirements. Complications may arise, however, as the property will appreciate in the future. This complex problem is considered in the next section.

12.3.1 Property Revaluations

Two extreme cases need to be considered: firstly, that where the bank already has and is anticipated to have all the secondary capital it can use, and, secondly, where the bank has a shortage of secondary capital. Intermediate cases would be an appropriate mixture of the two extremes. The first situation is illustrated in Table 12.5, which shows the group's balance sheets incremental to Table 12.4.

As always the easiest aspect is considered first. The subsidiary's assets increase £10m as a result of the revaluation, while the parent's investment in its subsidiary increases £10.8m, which consists of the revaluation itself plus the 8 per cent capital needed to support the extra value of the property. Group assets increase by £10m.

By assumption the bank has surplus second tier capital. Nevertheless the extra £10m of assets must be supported by additional equity. If the

TABLE 12.5 Impact of Property Revaluations (£m)

	Group	Parent	Sub.		Group	Parent	Sub.
Equity	0.50	0.50	0.80	Assets	10.00	–	10.00
Revaluation reserve	–	–	10.00	Subsidiary		10.80	
Capital	0.50	0.50	10.80				
Revaluation	10.00	10.00					
Subordinated debt	(10.00)	(10.00)					
Deposits	10.00	10.00					
	10.50	10.50	10.80				
Deposits	(0.50)	0.30	(0.80)				
	10.00	10.80	10.00		10.00	10.80	10.00

capital ratio is 10 per cent, then the extra equity must be at least 5 per cent, since second tier capital cannot exceed first tier capital; consequently equity increases £0.5m. The revaluation reserve could, in the absence of a surplus, count as second tier capital. Therefore it is used to replace subordinated debt which is more expensive than deposits.

Deposits increase £10m to make up the funding previously supplied by the subordinated debt. However, at the consolidated level the extra equity of £0.5m also replaces deposits, so that their net increase is £9.5m. The parent, however, has to make £0.8m of capital available to its subsidiary, so that the parent's deposits increase £10.3m. The subsidiary's deposits fall £0.8m, reflecting the £0.8m injection of endowed equity (or capital).

Thus the net cost of the revaluation to the parent is:

$$0.50r + 0.30i - 10di$$

or:

$$0.50(r-i) + 0.80i - 10di$$

or, more generally:

$$IE(r-i) + EEi - \text{Revaluation } di$$

It should be noted that the revaluation reserve is excluded from endowed equity, as it is only a book-keeping item which does not require

Evaluating Fixed Asset Expenditure

funding. In addition remember that the subsidiary's deposits have fallen £0.8m, with a consequent reduction in its costs. These costs, alongside the initial costs shown in expression 12.1, have to be set against rents saved to see whether it is worth investing in the property.

12.3.2 Property Revaluation: Insufficient Secondary Capital

Sometimes banks will be short of second tier capital, given a reluctance, or inability, to issue hybrid instruments. This section explores the financial consequences when this situation occurs. First, the situation before revaluing a subsidiary's property is shown in Table 12.6.

TABLE 12.6   Group Balance Sheets before Revaluation (£m)

	Group	Parent	Sub.		Group	Parent	Sub.
Equity	66.70	66.70	9.60	Loans	980.00	880.00	100.00
Subordinated debt	33.30	33.30	–	Premises	20.00	–	20.00
Revaluation	–	–	–	Subsidiary	–	9.60	–
Total capital	100.00	100.00	9.60				
Deposits	900.00	789.60	110.40				
	1000.00	889.60	120.00		1000.00	889.60	120.00

On the assets side of the balance sheets the subsidiary has £100m of loans and property costing £20m. The parent has loans in its own right of £880m. It has to endow its subsidiary with £9.6m of capital to allow the latter to satisfy local capital requirement of 8 per cent. At the consolidated level total assets amount to £1,000m.

Turning to liabilities, the subsidiary has £9.6m of equity, the balance of its assets being funded by local deposits of £110.4m. The UK bank operates subject to a 10 per cent capital requirement. Owing to limitations on secondary capital, the £100m capital is split two to one, equity to subordinated debt. General provisions have been ignored to ease exposition. Consolidated deposits are £900m, and by difference the parent's deposits are £789.6m.

It is now necessary to examine the financial impact of a property revaluation. Table 12.7 shows the consequential balance sheets.

As a consequence of the revaluation, total group assets and capital increase £10m and £1m respectively, compared with Table 12.6. From

FINANCIAL DECISION-MAKING

TABLE 12.7 Group Balance Sheets after Revaluation (£m)

	Group	Parent	Sub.		Group	Parent	Sub.
Equity	60.70	60.70	10.40	Loans	980.00	880.00	100.00
Subordinated debt	30.30	30.30	–	Property	20.00	–	20.00
Revaluation	10.00	10.00	10.00	Revaluation	10.00	–	10.00
Capital	101.00	101.00	20.40	Subsidiary	–	20.40	–
Deposits	909.00	799.40	109.60				
	1010.00	900.40	130.00		1010.00	900.40	130.00

total capital of £101m, the revaluation of £10m can be deducted. Thus only £91m of capital needs to be provided by equity and subordinated debt in the ratio two to one.

Compared with Table 12.6, the benefits to the parent are a £6m reduction in imputed equity and a £3m fall in subordinated debt. Offsetting these gains, the parent's deposits increase £9.8m, i.e. the £9m reduction in equity and subordinated debt, and the extra £0.8m of endowed equity required by the subsidiary. More formally the benefit is:

$6r + 3(i+di) - 9.8i$

More generally the following can be stated:

- Total capital, excluding the revaluation, falls by the revaluation less the extra capital needed to support the revaluation.
- This fall in capital releases equity and subordinated debt in the ratio two to one.
- The parent's deposits increase by the reduction in original capital, plus the increase in the subsidiary's endowed equity.

In addition the subsidiary's deposits fall by £0.8m, the increase in its endowed equity. This increase will also be subject to an FX holding gain or loss.

12.3.3 Sale of Premises

To judge whether it is worthwhile retaining premises it is necessary to examine the consequences of selling and then renting. Table 12.8 explores the balance sheet implications, in the case where there is an insufficiency of second tier capital.

[138]

Evaluating Fixed Asset Expenditure

TABLE 12.8 Sale of Premises (£m)

	Group	Parent	Sub.		Group	Parent	Sub.
Equity	65.30	65.30	8.00	Loans	980.00	880.00	100.00
Subordinated debt	32.70	32.70	–	Property	–	–	–
Revaluation				Revaluation	–	–	–
Capital	98.00	98.00	8.00	Subsidiary	–	8.00	–
Deposits	882.00	790.00	92.00				
	980.00	888.00	100.00		980.00	888.00	100.00

Compared to Table 12.7, total assets have fallen £30m, so that the capital needed by the parent falls £3m. At the same time the parent's deposits have fallen £9.4m, consisting of the £12.4m decline in the parent's assets, offset by the £3m fall in its capital. However, because the £10m revaluation reserve has been paid out to shareholders, the bank needs an additional £7m of capital in the ratio two to one of equity to subordinated debt. Therefore the net gain on sale, compared to the situation shown in Table 12.7, is:

$$(10.0 - 4.6)r - 2.4(i + di) + 9.4i$$

In the equity flows the net release of equity would be shown as a one-off gain. In addition the subsidiary's deposits have fallen £17.6m. It should be noted that any capital gains tax liability resulting from the sale has been ignored; any such liability should be deducted from the benefits.

12.3.4 Two Examples

Initially the consequences of retaining premises, when there is insufficient second tier capital, are examined in Table 12.9. The implications of sale are explored next in Table 12.10. The first part of Table 12.9 shows the local balance sheet and profit and loss account (rows 1 to 8). The only asset considered is premises, since it is assumed that all other assets remain the same before and after the property is sold. However, if local liquidity requirements are onerous, the supporting balance sheet should be constructed. The initial value of the property is USD100m; its value increases 5 per cent every year.

On the liabilities side of the balance sheet equity consists of two elements. It is assumed that the local regulator requires the market value

FINANCIAL DECISION-MAKING

TABLE 12.9 Evaluation of Retention of Premises

			Year 1	2	3	4	5	23	24	25
	Assets									
1	Premises	1.050	100.00	105.00	110.25	115.76	121.55	292.53	307.15	322.51
	Endowed equity:									
2	Premises		8.00	8.40	8.82	9.26	9.72	23.40	24.57	25.80
3	Reval. res.		40.00	45.00	50.25	55.76	61.55	232.53	247.15	262.51
4	Deposits		48.00	53.40	59.07	65.02	71.27	255.93	271.72	288.31
			52.00	51.60	51.18	50.74	50.28	36.60	35.43	34.20
			100.00	105.00	110.25	115.76	121.55	292.53	307.15	322.51
5	Profit and loss account									
6	Cost of deposits	0.100	(5.20)	(5.16)	(5.12)	(5.07)	(5.03)	(3.66)	(3.54)	(3.42)
7	TAX at	0.400	2.08	2.06	2.05	2.03	2.01	1.46	1.42	1.37
8	PAT		(3.12)	(3.10)	(3.07)	(3.04)	(3.02)	(2.20)	(2.13)	(2.05)
9	Parent's balance sheet									
10	Banking assets		10,000.00	10,000.00	10,000.00	10,000.00	10,000.00	10,000.00	10,000.00	10,000.00
11	Investment in subsidiary		24.00	29.67	31.93	34.22	37.33	123.02	129.99	137.27
			10,024.00	10,029.67	10,031.93	10,034.22	10,037.33	10,123.02	10,129.99	10,137.27
12	Cash equity		656.67	653.44	652.21	650.97	649.25	602.01	598.17	594.17
13	Holding gain		0.00	0.44	0.32	0.19	0.17	(0.48)	(0.54)	(0.59)
14	Equity		656.67	653.89	652.53	651.16	649.42	601.53	597.64	593.58
15	Subordinated debt		328.33	326.94	326.27	325.58	324.71	300.76	298.82	296.79
16	Revaluation		20.00	25.00	27.16	29.35	32.24	111.77	118.24	124.99
17	Total capital		1,005.00	1,005.83	1,005.96	1,006.09	1,006.37	1,014.06	1,014.69	1,015.36
18	Deposits		9,019.00	9,023.83	9,025.97	9,028.13	9,030.97	9,108.96	9,115.30	9,121.91
			10,024.00	10,029.67	10,031.93	10,034.22	10,037.33	10,123.02	10,129.99	10,137.27
19	Annual holding gain		0.00	0.44	(0.13)	(0.13)	(0.02)	(0.05)	(0.05)	(0.06)
	FX	2.000	1.80	1.85	1.90	1.91	1.92	2.09	2.10	2.11
	UK inflation	1.045								
	Foreign inflation	1.050								
20	Equity flows GBP									
21	PAT foreign		(1.73)	(1.67)	(1.62)	(1.59)	(1.57)	(1.05)	(1.01)	(0.97)
	PAT UK	(656.67)	(586.24)	(586.55)	(586.69)	(586.83)	(587.01)	(592.08)	(592.49)	(592.92)
22	Imputed equity		3.22	1.23	1.24	1.72	1.79	3.83	4.00	4.18
23	Int. on sub. debt		(22.41)	(22.31)	(22.27)	(22.22)	(22.16)	(20.53)	(20.39)	(20.26)
		(656.67)	(607.15)	(609.31)	(609.33)	(608.92)	(608.95)	(609.83)	(609.90)	(609.97)
	NPV at	0.140	(4,841.792)							

[140]

Evaluating Fixed Asset Expenditure

of the property to be supported by total capital of 8 per cent. Since the UK bank is assumed to endow its subsidiary with the full amount, interest-free, it can be treated as endowed equity. In addition the revaluation reserves have to be included to match the difference between the value of the property and its original cost. The balance of liabilities is made up by locally funded deposits.

The profit and loss account just reflects the cost of deposits, which are offset by a 40 per cent tax credit.

For ease of exposition dummy accounts for the UK parent are constructed (rows 9 to 18). The parent's own assets are arbitrarily taken to be £10bn, and varying them makes no difference to the retention versus sales option. Alternatively the parent's assets could be put to zero, which allows the benefits of retention and sale to be calculated in their own right. The parent's investment in its subsidiary completes the asset side of its balance sheet. This side is the subsidiary's total endowed equity, which is USD48m at the beginning of year 1, or, on conversion to sterling, £24m (row 11).

The UK bank's consolidated capital ratio is 10 per cent. Total consolidated assets consist of the parent's directly held assets of £10bn, plus the subsidiary's premises. At the beginning of year 1 the latter is USD100m, or £50m. Therefore at the beginning of the evaluation period the total capital required by the UK bank is £1.005bn (row 17). Capital consists of the revaluation reserve, which is initially worth USD40m or £20m, plus equity and subordinated debt. There is, by assumption, a shortage of second tier capital, so that the balance of capital is split between equity and subordinated debt in the ratio of two to one (rows 14 and 15). General provisions have been ignored for simplicity of exposition. The balance of liabilities is made up by deposits.

Equity itself consists of two elements, 'holding gain' and 'cash equity' (rows 13 and 14). Holding gain enables dividends to be increased without impacting on the bank's cash equity. Consequently only the latter is a direct cost to shareholders and used in the equity flows (row 22).

Foreign profits (row 20) are the cost of deposits less tax at 40 per cent converted to sterling. UK profits are the cost of the UK parent's deposits net of tax at 35 per cent. Income from the parent's assets has been excluded, for it cancels out with the parent's income in the property sale case, and so is irrelevant to the relative merits of retention and sale. Interest on subordinated debt is 10.5 per cent less UK tax.

With all these assumptions the net equity flows generate a negative NPV of £4,841.8m, when discounted at 14 per cent.

Table 12.10 shows the same information following the sale of the premises. The subsidiary now has no assets or liabilities, but rent is

FINANCIAL DECISION-MAKING

TABLE 12.10 Evaluation of Sale of Premises

		Year 1	2	3	4	5	23	24	25
	Assets								
1	Premises	1.050	0.00	0.00	0.00	0.00	0.00	0.00	0.00
	Profit and loss account								
2	Rent	1.050	(7.50)	(7.88)	(8.27)	(8.68)	(9.12)	(21.94)	(23.04)	(24.19)
3	PBT		(7.50)	(7.88)	(8.27)	(8.68)	(9.12)	(21.94)	(23.04)	(24.19)
4	TAX at	0.400	3.00	3.15	3.31	3.47	3.65	8.78	9.21	9.68
5	PAT		(4.50)	(4.73)	(4.96)	(5.21)	(5.47)	(13.16)	(13.82)	(14.51)
	Parent's balance sheet								
6	Banking assets		10,000.00	10,000.00	10,000.00	10,000.00	10,000.00	10,000.00	10,000.00	10,000.00
7	Investment in subsidiary		0.00	0.00	0.00	0.00	0.00	0.00	0.00	0.00
			10,000.00	10,000.00	10,000.00	10,000.00	10,000.00	10,000.00	10,000.00	10,000.00
8	Equity		666.67	666.67	666.67	666.67	666.67	666.67	666.67	666.67
9	Subordinated debt		333.33	333.33	333.33	333.33	333.33	333.33	333.33	333.33
10	Revaluation		0.00	0.00	0.00	0.00	0.00	0.00	0.00	0.00
11	Total capital		1,000.00	1,000.00	1,000.00	1,000.00	1,000.00	1,000.00	1,000.00	1,000.00
12	Deposits		9,000.00	9,000.00	9,000.00	9,000.00	9,000.00	9,000.00	9,000.00	9,000.00
			10,000.00	10,000.00	10,000.00	10,000.00	10,000.00	10,000.00	10,000.00	10,000.00
	FX	2.000	1.80	1.85	1.90	1.91	1.92	2.09	2.10	2.11
	UK inflation	1.045								
	Foreign inflation	1.050								
13	Equity flows GBP		(2.50)	(2.55)	(2.61)	(2.73)	(2.85)	(6.30)	(6.58)	(6.88)
14	PAT foreign		(585.00)	(585.00)	(585.00)	(585.00)	(585.00)	(585.00)	(585.00)	(585.00)
	PAT UK	20.00								
15	Revaluation surplus	(666.67)	0.00	0.00	0.00	0.00	0.00	0.00	0.00	0.00
16	Imputed equity		(22.75)	(22.75)	(22.75)	(22.75)	(22.75)	(22.75)	(22.75)	(22.75)
17	Int. on sub. debt									
		(646.67)	(610.25)	(610.30)	(610.36)	(610.48)	(610.60)	(614.05)	(614.33)	(614.63)
NPV at	0.140	(4,846.138)	NPV retention less NPV sale 4.35							

[142]

Evaluating Fixed Asset Expenditure

incurred at 7.5 per cent of the property's market value. The net of tax cost is shown in row 5.

The proceeds from the sale of the premises are used, firstly, to pay a dividend of £20m, that being the revaluation surplus. The balance of £30m is used in effect to reduce the parent's deposits. Now the parent's, and indeed the group's, only assets are the £10bn of directly held assets. With a 10 per cent capital ratio total capital falls £5m, to £1bn. The latter has to be split between equity and debt in the ratio two to one, as there is no revaluation surplus (rows 8, 9 and 10). Opening imputed equity of £666.67m is the equity cost of the business, and is shown in row 16 of the equity flows.

Foreign profits, shown in row 13 of the equity flows, are the sterling cost of the subsidiary's rent. UK profits are the net of tax cost of the parent's deposits. The cost of subordinated debt is given in row 17.

The equity flows to the group following the premises sale, when discounted at 14 per cent, give a negative NPV of £4,846.1m. Thus on comparing the NPVs of the two situations, it is seen that retention is better by a NPV of £4.4m.

To keep the exposition straightforward, several assumptions have been made. No capital gains tax has been charged; it could be up to 35 per cent of the revaluation surplus, and can be significant.

In the retention case initial holding gains were zero, but in practice this will not be the case. However, such gains can be ignored, as their opening level will be the same in both options.

The particular example considered assumed that there was a shortage of second tier capital, but this may not be the case. Nevertheless the two examples provide a suitable framework to evaluate retention and sale options when there is a sufficiency of second tier capital. The appropriate balance sheet structure will be based upon the discussion in section 12.3.2.

Annex

Revaluations Contribute to First Tier Capital

At the end of February 1989 National Westminster Bank announced its results for 1988. However, far more interest was caused by its scrip issue, which capitalised part of its property revaluation surpluses. While, on the face of it, contrary to the BIS rules, it appears that the conversion will be allowed to count as first tier capital. Midland Bank subsequently followed suit.

The implications are similar to the treatment of FX holding gains. Property revaluations can now count towards equity for capital adequacy purposes. Shareholders do not contribute to this source of equity, which can be used to boost dividends without impairing capital ratios, as Table 12.11 shows.

TABLE 12.11 Revaluation Reserves Treated as Equity (£m)

	Before Revaluation	After Revaluation
Assets		
Lending	95.00	95.00
Property	5.00	6.00
	100.00	101.00
Equity	5.00	4.05
Revaluation reserve	–	1.00
Second tier	5.00	5.05
Total first and second tiers	10.00	10.10
Deposits	90.00	90.90
	100.00	101.00

The bank operates with a total first and second tier capital ratio of 10 per cent, half of which is equity. Before the revaluation lending assets are £95m and property is shown at its initial £5m value. Following the revaluation of £1m, total assets increase to £101m. Total equity, including the revaluation reserve of £1m, increases to £5.05m, while total capital is assumed to increase to £10.1m.

Thus the bank has been able to distribute £0.95m in dividends, i.e. £5m less

Evaluating Fixed Asset Expenditure

£4.05m. At the same time its funding needs have also increased £0.95m, consisting of a £0.05m increase in second tier capital and a £0.90m increase in deposits. The interest that has to be paid on these funds partly offsets the benefits obtained by the shareholders.

13

PRICING

13.1 Rationale

A pricing model is used to determine the product prices necessary to achieve a target rate of return on the equity needed to support delivery of the product. Costs can be standard costs, which assume full recovery of all costs at standard levels of activity. Alternatively marginal costs can be used if there is significant under-utilised capacity. Whatever the result, such models only provide guidance. If they result in prices higher than those charged, this may indicate that the marketing team have been doing a poor job, and that prices should be increased; or the results may indicate that costs are too high. It may, however, just be impossible to earn an acceptable return on the product.

All too often the desired price will be higher than the market will accept. Various options are available. The product can be withdrawn either immediately, or gradually, by setting the full cost price and then losing business. In itself this might not solve anything, for shared overheads will have to be borne by other products and as a result they may no longer be profitable. Other avenues can be explored. As well as determining full cost prices the model can be used to examine cost levels that will generate the required return on equity, given likely market prices. Unit costs can be reduced by rationalisation or by increased sales at market-determined prices.

The profitability or margins required on groups of products can be analysed. Exactly the same methodology can be used to estimate customer profitability, and what is necessary to improve it. Ultimately the return to an operation can be considered along with all the options to improve it.

13.2 The Supporting Balance Sheet Revisited

A promise was made in the introduction only to make use of the simplest algebra. So far this promise has been kept, and the mathematics used has

Pricing

required little effort to comprehend. It is now impossible to avoid the introduction of little more algebra. While it may, to the layman, seem a little daunting, there is really not that much to it. Line by line explanations combined with a little diligence will see the most innumerate reader through.

Pricing models are very common, but all too often not enough thought is given to them. They are based on the accounting relation between revenue, costs and profit: profit plus cost equals revenue, where profit is the required return on equity, and revenue is the sum of profit and costs. Take a commercial loan as an example, and assume that the required yield or margin is to be derived. Let the value of the loan be 100 units of currency, say £100, which has the advantage that all results are automatically percentages. Further assume that the capital RWA ratio is 8 per cent, the lowest allowed under BIS, and that there is no shortage of second tier capital. With a 15 per cent COE the profit after tax required on the £4 of equity is £0.6. The profit and loss account would take the form shown in Table 13.1.

TABLE 13.1 Pricing: Profit and Loss Account (£m)

Required profit	0.60	Revenue	13.12
Cost of second tier debt (at 10.5%)	0.42		
Cost of Deposits (at 10.0%)	9.20		
Operating costs	2.50		
Tax (at 40%)	0.40		
Total costs	13.12		13.12

By assumption there is £4 of second tier capital, which costs £0.42m, £92 of deposits costing £9.2 and operating costs of £2.5. Local corporation tax is 40 per cent. With these assumptions the asset needs to yield 13.12 per cent, or a margin of 3.12 per cent in relation to deposits costing 10 per cent.

This is fine as far as it goes but a lot more is required. A subsidiary's pricing must reflect opportunity costs to the bank's parent, so that, just like project appraisals, allowances must be made for the interest adjustments on imputed and endowed equity. Further, the balance sheet consistent with the profit and loss account shown in Table 13.1 does not reflect the full reality of the situation. It only has the one asset, while liabilities only consist of deposits and capital. As explained in Chapter 12, regulators impose liquidity requirements on banks as well as capital constraints.

FINANCIAL DECISION-MAKING

Generally liquidity or reserve requirements relate to a bank's deposit base, and sometimes other liabilities are also included. In total they are called eligible liabilities. At the beginning of 1988 the Bank of Spain imposed the following requirements on banks operating in Spain:

Asset	Percentage of eligible liabilities	Remuneration
Cash with Bank of Spain	2.5	nil
Cash with Bank of Spain	16.0	7.75%
State debt	1.0	6.56%
Treasury Bills	10.0	5.88%

Eligible liabilities are defined by the Bank of Spain as deposits from the private sector (excluding interbank), repurchase agreements, bankers' acceptances and participations sold to third parties in loan assets. At the time money market rates were around 12 per cent, so the Bank of Spain's requirements imposed a considerable burden. Other central banks impose different types of liquidity constraints.

Clearly any pricing model must take account of reserve requirements when it imposes a significant cost. Likewise any fixed assets needed to support an activity must be taken into account. Some of these points are illustrated in Table 13.2.

To derive this table the following assumptions have been made. All liquidity ratios and yields on liquid assets are taken from the Spanish information, except that state debt and treasury bills are assumed to earn 6 per cent. Local equity is taken as 10 per cent of banking and fixed assets. Local profit tax is 35 per cent. UK imputed equity is 7 per cent of RWA, with 3 per cent second tier capital. Banking assets and fixed assets have a 100 per cent weighting. Spanish government instruments are given a 10 per cent weighting to reflect the interest rate risk. The COE is 14 per cent and interest, net of UK tax, on imputed and endowed equity is 6.5 per cent.

If the UK parent is to earn 14 per cent on its imputed equity, then total revenue earned on the asset must be £17.45. As the cost of local deposits is 12 per cent, the required margin is 5.45 per cent. It is quite likely that the market will not accept such a high margin. Perhaps 5 per cent is the most that can be obtained.

The model can be used to explore ways of achieving this rate. A reduction in costs to £2.05 would do the trick, i.e. £2.50 less £0.45, but it may not be possible to rationalise to this extent. Nevertheless, suppose there is considerable surplus capacity, that fixed costs amount to £1.25 and variable costs to £(1.25/100) × L, where L is the volume of lending.

Pricing

TABLE 13.2 Pricing a Loan (GBP)

Local balance sheet			
Endowed equity	10.30	Cash (0.0%)	3.29
Secondary capital	0.00	Cash (7.75%)	21.04
	10.30	Government debt (6%)	14.46
Deposits	131.49	Banking asset	100.00
		Fixed Assets	3.00
Total liabilities	141.79	Total Assets	141.79
Local profit and loss account			
Required ROIE (at 14%)	1.0236	Cash (0.0%)	0.0000
Deposits (at 12%)	15.7786	Cash (7.75%)	1.5779
Operating costs	2.5000	Government debt (6%)	0.8678
Int. endowed equity	0.0670	Int. imputed equity	0.0475
Second tier Adjustment	0.0102		2.4932
Local tax (35%)	0.5671	Revenue on asset	17.4533
Total costs	19.9465		19.9465

Assume lending increases from £100 to £156.25; then total costs will become £3.203, or 2.05 per cent of lending, and the COE will just be obtained. At the other extreme this analysis could be applied to the bank's balance sheet and profit and loss account to explore ways of achieving the COE.

13.3 Derivation of the Basic Model

To keep the procedure as straightforward as possible the model will be built up in stages. During the first stage only reserve assets in relation to deposits will be considered. Moreover the required relationships will be derived using only two reserve assets; the generalisation to three or more will then be apparent. First, the local balance sheet has to be developed; the procedure starts by considering local capital requirements. Thus define:

$$K = aW \qquad (13.1)$$

where K is the local capital requirement, W the locally determined RWA, and a the capital to RWAs ratio.

FINANCIAL DECISION-MAKING

Next the relation between reserve assets 1 and 2 must be formalised:

$$R(1) = r(1)D \quad (13.2)$$
$$R(2) = r(2)D \quad (13.3)$$

where $R(1)$ is reserve asset 1, $r(1)$ the ratio of reserve asset 1 to deposits, and D the total deposits.

And similarly for reserve asset 2.

Equation 13.2 can be rewritten:

$$D = R(1)/r(1) \quad (13.4)$$

Substituting the RHS of the above for D in equation 13.3 gives:

$$R(2) = \frac{r(2)}{r(1)} R(1) \quad (13.5)$$

From the equality of balance sheet assets and liabilities it can be stated that deposits equal total assets less capital and any other liabilities. More formally:

$$D = A(R) + A(0) - K \quad (13.6)$$

where $A(R)$ are the total reserve assets and $A(0)$ all other assets.

Substituting the RHS of 13.6 for D in equation 13.2 gives:

$$R(1) = r(1)[A(R) + A(0) - K] \quad (13.7)$$

Replacing $A(R)$ by the two reserve assets gives:

$$R(1) = r(1)[R(1) + R(2) + A(0) - K]$$

Replace $R(2)$ in the above by the RHS of equation 13.5 to give:

$$R(1) = r(1)[R(1) + \frac{r(2)}{r(1)} R(1) + A(0) - K] \quad (13.8)$$

Assume that the bank only has one asset other than its reserve assets, and that it has a risk weighting $w(3)$. Further assume that reserve assets 1 and 2 have risk weightings $w(1)$ and $w(2)$ respectively. From equation 13.1 total capital becomes:

[150]

Pricing

$$K = a[w(1)R(1) + w(2)R(2) + w(3)A(0)] \quad \quad \quad (13.9)$$

Substituting the RHS of 13.5 for $R(2)$ in 13.9, the latter becomes:

$$K = a[w(1)R(1) + w(2)\frac{r(2)}{r(1)}R(1) + w(3)A(0)] \quad \quad (13.10)$$

On substituting the above expression for K into equation 13.8, the latter becomes:

$$R(1) = r(1)[R(1) + \frac{r(2)}{r(1)}R(1) + A(0) - a(w(1)R(1) + w(2)\frac{r(2)}{r(1)}R(1)$$
$$+ w(3)A(0))] \quad \quad \quad (13.11)$$

On rearranging the terms of 13.11, it becomes:

$$R(1) = r(1)[R(1)[1 + \frac{r(2)}{r(1)} - aw(1) - aw(2)\frac{r(2)}{r(1)}]$$
$$+ A(0)(1-aw(3))] \quad \quad \quad (13.12)$$

Bringing all the terms in $R(1)$ to the LHS of 13.12 gives:

$$R(1)[1 - r(1) - r(2) + aw(1)r(1) + aw(2)r(2)] = r(1)[A(0)(1-aw(3)] \quad \quad \quad (13.13)$$

All the terms in equation 13.13 are known apart from $R(1)$. Once 13.13 is solved for $R(1)$, equation 13.2 can be used to derive deposits, D. Once deposits are known, 13.3 can be used to obtain $R(2)$. Although $R(1)$ has been derived by using only two reserve assets and one other asset, the generalisation to any number of assets is easily done.

The first three terms on the LHS of equation 13.13 are $1 - r(1) - r(2)$. With n reserve assets this term is simply extended to become:

$$1 - r(1) - r(2) - r(3) - \ldots - r(n)$$

and the last two terms on the LHS side of 13.13 are $a[w(1)r(1) + w(2)r(2)]$. Again on increasing the number of reserve assets to n this expression generalises to:

$$a[w(1)r(1) + w(2)r(2) + w(3)r(3) + + w(n)r(n)]$$

FINANCIAL DECISION-MAKING

where $r(i)$ is the ratio of reserve asset i to deposits and $w(i)$ the risk weighting applied to asset i.

As well as the n reserve assets suppose there were k other assets. In this case the RHS of 13.13 generalises to:

$$r(1)[A(1)(1 - aw(n+1)) + A(2)(1 - aw(n+2)) + \ldots + A(k)(1 - aw(n+k))]$$

where $A(j)$ is the jth non-reserve asset and $w(n+j)$ the risk weighting of the above asset.

A further generalisation is still necessary. In defining the level of local capital required in equation 13.9 risk-weighted contingents were ignored in order to keep the process as simple as possible. If there are m of these with risk weightings $w(n+k+1)$ to $w(n+k+m)$, then required capital increases by:

$$a[w(n+k+1)C(n+k+1) + \ldots + w(n+k+m)C(n+k+m)]$$

where $C(n+k+1)$ denotes the first of the contingent liabilities.

When this extra term is inserted into equation 13.10, and through it into 13.11, the following has to be added to the RHS of 13.13.

$$- r(1)a[w(n+k+1)C(n+k+1) + \ldots + w(n+k+m)C(n+k+m)]$$

Deposits have been treated as homogeneous. In practice they are hetrogeneous and this is sometimes reflected in the liquidity requirements imposed by regulators. This causes no problems. The Central Bank might require all deposits maturing within a week to be supported by 10 per cent cash. These deposits may typically account for 25 per cent of all deposits, so that the cash ratio would be 2.5 per cent with respect to all deposits, and would be used in equation 13.13.

Revaluation reserves caused problems when evaluating whether or not to own premises; in this context they cause none. Such reserves are not funded, and for the purpose of modelling can be treated as though they were a contingent liability.

Taxation can only be indirectly derived from the profit and loss account. Ignoring differences between depreciation charges and tax allowances, local tax is simply the rate of profits tax applied to local profits, that is:

$$T = [R - C + C(N)]t \qquad (13.14)$$

Pricing

where T is the profits tax, t the local tax rate, R all revenues, C all costs, and $C(N)$ costs not allowed against tax.

Next it is necessary to obtain a relation between return on imputed equity ROIE and profits tax, and this is shown below:

$$\text{ROIE} = [R - C - T - \text{EE}i + \text{IE}i] \quad\quad\quad (13.15)$$

With regard to Table 13.2, the above relationship just restates, in a formal way, the profit and loss account. In other words, the post-tax return on imputed equity must equal all revenues, less expenses and taxes, to give local profits after tax. Local profits are then subject to the normal interest adjustments on endowed and imputed equity.

Rearranging equation 13.15, to show revenue only on the RHS, gives:

$$[\text{ROIE} + C + T + \text{EE}i - \text{IE}i] = R$$

Substituting the above expression for R into equation 13.14 gives:

$$T = [\text{ROIE} + C + T + \text{EE}i - \text{IE}i - C + C(N)]t$$

so that:

$$T = [\text{ROIE} + T + \text{EE}i - \text{E}i + C(N)]t$$

and:

$$T[1-t] = [\text{ROIE} + \text{EE}i - \text{IE}i + C(N)]t$$

and:

$$T = \frac{t}{(1-t)} [\text{ROIE} + \text{EE}i - \text{IE}i + C(N)] \quad\quad (13.16)$$

All items on the RHS of 13.16 are known. Imputed equity, and hence the ROIE, can be calculated from the balance sheet which has already been derived, and similarly for endowed equity. The tax rate is known, and so is the net of tax UK interest rate applied to endowed and imputed equity. The foreign subsidiary may be endowed with second tier capital as well as equity, but the same interest rate adjustment applies to the former as to the latter and it can simply be added to endowed equity in all the above relations. Likewise the differential interest on second tier capital, shown as the second tier adjustment in Table 13.2, can be shown as a deduction in equation 13.15.

Required revenue, that is the 'Revenue on asset' shown in Table 13.2, can be plugged in to equate both sides of the profit and loss account. Alternatively, as a check on the alegebra, equation 13.14 can be used to calculate required revenue. Both sides of the profit and loss account will equate if the algebra is correct. Thus rearranging 13.14, gives:

$$Rt = T + Ct - C(N)t$$

that is:

$$R = [T + Ct - C(N)t]\frac{1}{t}$$

where T is taken from equation 13.16.

Remember, however, that the revenue in the above equation is total local revenue. In Table 13.2 it includes income generated by the reserve assets, and this income must be deducted from R to obtain the income that the asset being priced must generate. Moreover the model might be used to examine relation profitability. In this case other income would be an input into the model, and this too should be deducted.

13.4 Extension of the Model

Required liquidity has only been related to deposits. As the Spanish example shows, liquidity can be related to certain types of contingent liabilities, while in a few countries liquidity may also relate to specific assets. This section developes the model to incorporate these complications. Again a certain amount of algebra cannot be avoided, but it will be introduced carefully and in enough stages to allow it to be followed easily.

This section starts off with equation 13.1, but equations 13.2 and 13.3 are replaced by new ones which add the relationship between liquid, or reserve, assets on the one hand and contingents and assets on the other. All of this could have been tackled in the previous section, but it should be easier for the less mathematically inclined reader to follow this route. As before, the process starts off with equation 13.1. Equations 13.2 and 13.3 are replaced by the following:

Pricing

$$R(1) = r(1)D + Z(1) \qquad (13.17)$$

$$R(2) = r(2)D + Z(2) \qquad (13.18)$$

The only difference is the addition of the terms $Z(1)$ and $Z(2)$. They denote the relation between reserve or liquid assets, on the one hand, and the bank's contingents and assets, on the other. To keep the algebra straightforward, this relation will be spelt out at the end of this section. For the moment only, take it on trust.

From equation 13.17, deposits D can be expressed in terms of the other items, so:

$$D = [R(1) - Z(1)] \frac{1}{r(1)} \qquad (13.19)$$

Using the above relation for D, and substituting it into 13.18, we have:

$$R(2) = \frac{r(2)}{r(1)}[R(1) - Z(1)] + Z(2) \qquad (13.20)$$

Using equation 13.6 for deposits D, equation 13.17 becomes:

$$R(1) = r(1)[A(R) + A(0) - K] + Z(1)$$

Remembering that $A(R) = R(1) + R(2)$, the above becomes:

$$R(1) = r(1)[R(1) + R(2) + A(0) - K] + Z(1) \qquad (13.21)$$

Replace $R(2)$ in 13.21 by the RHS of equation 13.20, to obtain:

$$R(1) = r(1)\,[R(1) + \frac{r(2)}{r(1)}[R(1) - Z(1)] + Z(2)$$

$$+ A(0) - K] + Z(1) \qquad (13.22)$$

Replace K in 13.22 by the RHS of equation 13.9, to get:

$$R(1) = r(1)\,[R(1) + \frac{r(2)}{r(1)}[R(1) - Z(1)] + Z(2) + A(0)$$

$$- a(w(1)R(1) + w(2)R(2) + w(3)A(0))] + Z(1) \qquad (13.23)$$

FINANCIAL DECISION-MAKING

$R(2)$ in the above can again be replaced by the RHS of 13.20, to give:

$$R(1) = r(1)\,[R(1) + \frac{r(2)}{r(1)}\,[R(1) - Z(1)] + Z(2) + A(0)]$$
$$- r(1)a[w(1)R(1) + w(2)[\frac{r(2)}{r(1)}\,((R(1) - Z(1)) + Z(2)]$$
$$+ w(3)A(0))] + Z(1) \quad \dots\dots\dots\dots\dots\dots\dots\dots \quad (13.24)$$

All terms involving $R(1)$ are now brought to the LHS of 13.24.

$$R(1)[1 - r(1) - r(2) + aw(1)r(1) + aw(2)r(2)] \text{ equals}$$
$$-r(2)Z(1) + r(1)Z(2) + r(1)A(0) + ar(2)w(2)Z(1) - aw(2)r(1)Z(2)$$
$$-r(1)aw(3)A(0) + Z(1) \quad \dots\dots\dots\dots\dots\dots\dots\dots \quad (13.25)$$

Regrouping the terms on the RHS, gives:

$$R(1)[1 - r(1) - r(2) + aw(1)r(1) + aw(2)r(2)] \text{ equals}$$
$$r(1)[A(0)(1-aw(3)] + Z(1)[1 - r(2) + ar(2)w(2)] + Z(2)[r(1) - aw(2)r(1)] \quad \dots\dots\dots\dots\dots\dots\dots\dots \quad (13.26)$$

The LHS of equation 13.26 is no different from that of equation 13.13; nor is the first expression on the RHS any different from the RHS of 13.13. Only the last two terms in $Z(1)$ and $Z(2)$ are different. Take the first of these, which is unique to $Z(1)$ and can be rewritten:

$$Z(1)[1+r(2)[aw(2)-1]$$

The term $r(2)[aw(2) - 1]$ is associated with reserve asset 2. Had there been three or more reserve assets, additional and exactly similar terms would be required. Thus with n reserve assets the term becomes:

$$Z(1)[1 + r(2)[aw(2) - 1] + \ldots + r(n)[aw(n) - 1]]$$

The third expression on the RHS of 13.26, which involves $Z(2)$, can be rewritten:

$$r(1)[Z(2)(1 - aw(2))]$$

Again there is only one term because there were only two reserve assets. With n reserve assets this expression would expand to:

[156]

Pricing

$$r(1)[z(2)[1-aw(2)]+ \ldots + Z(n)[1-aw(n)]]$$

Equation 13.26 is now quite general, apart from specifying the nature of the $Z(j)$. Each $Z(j)$ shows how reserve asset j is related to contingents and assets. By way of example, suppose that contingents 7 and 8 must be supported by 5 per cent and 10 per cent of reserve asset j. Likewise assume asset 5 must be supported by 7.5 per cent of reserve asset j. In this case $Z(j)$ becomes:

$$Z(j) = 0.050C(7) + 0.100C(8) + 0.075A(5).$$

All this may appear very complicated, but it took little more than a day to set it up on a PC. And the effort is well worthwhile.

13.5 Fee Income

Bankers often take the view that fee income is preferable to interest income, though there is no evidence to support this stance. Fee income can only be generated with the aid of plant equipment, premises and in many cases risk-weighted contingents. All of these must be backed by equity and second tier capital. Moreover fee income is generally associated with much higher cost income ratios than interest income. As well as rewarding equity these higher costs must be recovered.

Two examples of pricing contingents will be considered: firstly, when no supporting reserve assets are required and, secondly, when they are. The first case is illustrated in Table 13.3, where a contingent, perhaps a guarantee, with a risk weighting of 1.0 is priced. Allocated fixed assets are still £3, and operating costs remain at £2.5. £10.3 of endowed equity is required to support £103 of risk-weighted assets. However, no deposits are needed to support the contingent liability, yet both sides of the balance sheet must equal each other. This can only be achieved by the introduction of negative deposits, in turn implying that reserve assets must be negative. Really this just means that this activity is lending its endowed equity to the rest of the bank.

This explanation can be confirmed by considering two activities jointly. Thus the lending shown in Table 13.2 can be combined with the contingent exposure of Table 13.3. Their combined impact should just be the sum of the individual revenues required. Table 13.4 confirms this, showing a total required revenue of £20.501.

TABLE 13.3 Pricing a Contingent (GBP)

Local balance sheet			
Endowed equity	10.30	Cash (0.0%)	(0.26)
Secondary capital	0.00	Cash (7.75%)	(1.65)
	10.30	Government debt (6%)	(1.14)
Deposits	(10.35)	Banking asset	0.00
		Fixed assets	3.00
Total liabilities	(0.05)	Total assets	(0.05)
Local profit and loss account			
Required ROIE (at 14%)	1.0083	Cash (0.0%)	0.0000
Deposits (at 12%)	(1.2426)	Cash (7.75%)	(0.1243)
Operating costs	2.5000	Government debt (6%)	(0.0683)
Specific provision	0.0000	Other income	0.0000
Int. endowed equity	0.0670	Imputed equity	0.0468
Second tier adj.	0.0100		−0.1458
Local tax (35%)	0.5592	Revenue on contingent	3.0477
Total costs	2.9019	Total revenue	2.9019

TABLE 13.4 Combined Pricing of Loans and Contingents (GBP)

Local balance sheet			
Endowed equity	20.60	Cash (0.0%)	3.03
Secondary capital	0.00	Cash (7.75%)	19.38
	20.60	Government debt (6%)	13.32
Deposits	121.13	Loans	100.00
		Fixed assets	6.00
Total liabilities	141.73	Total assets	141.73
Local profit and loss account			
Required ROIE	2.0319	Cash (0.0%)	0.0000
Deposits (at 12%)	14.5362	Cash (7.75%)	1.4536
Operating costs	5.0000	Government debt (6%)	0.7995
Specific provision	0.0000	Other income	0.0000
Int. end equity	0.1338	Imputed equity	0.0943
Second tier adj.	0.0202		2.3474
Local tax (35%)	1.1263	Revenue required	20.5010
Total costs	22.8484	Total revenue	22.8484

Pricing

It is worth noting that the fee income required of £3.05 is considerably less than the margin of £5.45 required on the loan. In this example the differential results from two factors: firstly, the contingent activity's loan to the rest of the bank, and, secondly, the high cost of reserve assets the loan is forced to support.

The latter point becomes clear when a repurchase agreement is priced. It has a weighting of 1.0, and under the Bank of Spain's liquidity requirements must be supported by reserve assets. In fact, as Table 13.5 shows when compared with Table 13.2, the contingent must be priced at the same rate as the loan. The corollary is obvious: contingents, other things being equal, can only be priced below loans when the former do not require reserve asset banking.

TABLE 13.5 Pricing of Contingent Requiring Reserve Assets (GBP)

Local balance sheet			
Endowed equity	10.30	Cash (0.0%)	3.29
Secondary capital	0.00	Cash (7.75%)	21.04
	10.30	Government debt (6.0%)	14.46
Deposits	31.49	Fixed assets	3.00
Total liabilities	41.79	Total assets	41.79
Local profit and loss account			
Required ROIE	1.0236	Cash (0.0%)	0.0000
Deposits	3.7786	Cash (7.75%)	1.5779
Operating costs	2.5000	Government debt (6.0%)	0.8678
Specific provisions	0.0000	Imputed equity	0.0475
Int. endowed equity	0.0670		
Second tier adjustment	0.0102		2.4932
Local tax	0.5671	Revenue on asset	5.4533
Total costs	7.9465	Total revenue	7.9465

13.6 Average and Marginal Cost Pricing

13.6.1 *External Pricing*

Average cost pricing must prevail in the long run if the bank is to remain profitable; by definition prices less than this will fail to cover all costs, including the COE. Nevertheless marginal cost pricing is a subject of legitimate interest. There are two aspects to it: more commonly it concerns pricing products at less than average costs under circumstances of excess capacity, but, more importantly, it also concerns the bank's internal utilisation of its own resources.

Little needs to be said about the former. If excess lending capacity exists, then the costs of additional lending, or of any services where capacity is under-utilised, will be less than average costs. Indeed they may not materially differ from zero. In these circumstances no adjustments are required to the model, apart from inputting the appropriate marginal costs.

No doubt marginal cost pricing will on occasions be appropriate. Nevertheless the approach has significant dangers. One group of clients will be treated more favourably than others when services are provided at marginal costs, and such price discrimination, even when not illegal, can have harmful consequences. Information usually percolates through to the market. Other clients will demand similar concessions, and their goodwill is likely to evaporate. Moreover, as demand grows, it will prove difficult to increase prices, for clients may move to other banks if only out of umbrage.

13.6.2 *Internal Marginal Cost Pricing*

Internal marginal cost pricing is always necessary for efficient resource allocation. The principle is easy to state: the highest cost source of funds should be allocated to the least profitable assets or contingents. If the required return on equity is not achieved, and costs cannot be reduced, then profits can be increased by dropping the product. With the pricing model and a decent costing system, application of the principle is also straightforward.

Four sources of funds are shown in Table 13.6, ranging in cost (including collection costs) from 5 per cent to 10 per cent. There is limited availability of the cheaper three, whereas the most expensive money market source is, for practical purposes, in unlimited supply. Markets available to the bank consist of multinational corporations, middle-market companies, personal lending and credit-card lending. The amount of business available from these market segments is noted at the bottom of the table. Within the body of the table are shown the returns on equity that can be achieved at a given cost of funds.

Given a 14 per cent COE, all markets are profitable when the cost of funds is 7 per cent or less. But even though funds are available at 7 per cent

Pricing

TABLE 13.6   Internal Marginal Cost Pricing: ROE %

Cost of funds	MNC	MMC	PL	CCL	Funds available £m
5%	20.0	22.0	25.0	30.0	100
7%	15.0	17.0	20.0	25.0	50
8%	12.5	14.5	17.5	22.5	50
10%	7.5	9.5	12.5	17.5	Unlimited
Volume of business (£m)	100	150	100	50	

and 5 per cent, no lending should be made to multinationals, and only £50m should be lent to middle-market companies; £50m of the cheapest funds should be lent to credit-card customers and the remaining £50m should fund personal lending. The balance of the personal lending opportunities should be fully funded by the funds costing 7 per cent. Finally the £50m of 8 per cent funds should support lending to middle corporates. No other lending should be undertaken.

Fully meeting the potential demand from the middle market and multinationals entails borrowing £200m from the money market at 10 per cent. At this cost both middle corporates and multinationals give a ROE less than the required 14 per cent, so that the bank could not deploy these funds and earn an acceptable return for its shareholders. They would be better off investing the equity and earning 14 per cent elsewhere.

Suppose, however, the bank decided to allocate the £50m of 5 per cent funds to multinationals, and fund the credit-card business from the money market. Both activities will appear profitable but the Bank's value will still decline. In allocating £50m of the cheapest funds to multinationals the Bank will earn 20 per cent, but it will lose 30 per cent on lending to its credit-card customers. The net loss, so far, will be 10 per cent. However, the bank will now borrow £50m on the money markets to fund lending to credit-card holders, with which it will earn 17.5 per cent on its equity. Taking all gains and losses, the bank will, as a result of lending £50m to multinationals, earn 7.5 per cent on the equity employed. Its COE is 14 per cent, however, so investment will have a negative NPV and the bank's shareholder value will fall.

Any increase in lending to the middle market, and any lending to multinationals will generate a ROE of less than 14 per cent. Hence the bank's shareholder value will decline. Only if multinationals and middle corporates generate a ROE in excess of 14 per cent against money-market funds of 10 per cent is it worth lending, or increasing lending, to them.

13.6.3 The Cost of Funds

Often this will be pretty obvious, but not always. Money-market funds will nearly always be the most expensive. For all but the smallest banks, the cost of gathering them in will be very small in relation to volume, and it might even be possible to ignore it. This certainly cannot be done when estimating the costs of retail or corporate customer deposits. Interest paid on customer deposits may sometimes be relatively low, but the costs of gathering them in are not. The operating and capital costs must be added to the interest cost of such funds when allocating resources within the bank.

Different deposits sometimes have different reserve asset requirements, which too can affect their cost. For example, shorter-term deposits are generally subject to more severe liquidity requirements, which pushes up their cost relative to longer-term deposits. Such an increase should be reflected not only in pricing policy, but also in the treasury's funding policy. It will not always be apparent in these circumstances which is the most expensive source of funds. When there is ambiguity, product pricing will have to be based on two or more sources of funds. As soon as this is done, it will be apparent which is the most expensive, since it will impose the higher fee or margin.

13.7 Local and Domestic Returns

In Chapter 9 it was shown that the impact of FX changes on the sterling rate of return can be significant. No allowance has been made for this. Section 9.5 showed that these benefits consisted of two elements: the holding gain on opening endowed equity and FX gain on profits. At the cost of some complication, both these factors can be built into the pricing model.

In Table 13.2 both the FX and holding gains can be added into the revenue side of the profit and loss account. The required revenue on the asset will correspondingly decline. In its turn equation 13.15 will have to be modified, with the holding and FX gains becoming deductions on the RHS. The deduction for the holding gain is straightforward, since it is the FX movement applied to endowed equity, but the FX gain on profits is more complicated, since it is local profits multiplied by the FX movement, that is:

$$[R-C-T] \times \text{FX movement}$$

Pricing

There is another and perhaps more illuminating way to deal with the problem. This approach considers the theoretical relations between rates of return in local currency terms and the required return in sterling terms. Once the relation is established, the local currency return can then be used in the model instead of the required sterling return.

Table 13.7 shows the approach. The assumptions utilised are local and UK pre-tax interest rates of 5 per cent and 10 per cent respectively, with

TABLE 13.7 Local and UK Returns Compared

Local currency						
1 Imputed equity		50.000	50.000	50.000	50.000	50.000
2 Endowed equity		45.000	45.000	45.000	45.000	45.000
3 Local profit		8.000	8.000	8.000	8.000	8.000
4 Imputed equity credit		2.500	2.500	2.500	2.500	2.500
5 Endowed equity debit		(2.250)	(2.250)	(2.250)	(2.250)	(2.250)
6 Adjusted profit		8.250	8.250	8.250	8.250	8.250
7 Tax		(3.288)	(3.288)	(3.288)	(3.288)	(3.288)
8 Adjusted PAT		4.963	4.963	4.963	4.963	4.963
9 ROIE		9.925%	9.925%	9.925%	9.925%	9.925%
10 FX rates	3.5	3.341	3.189	3.044	2.906	2.774
Sterling						
11 Imputed equity		14.286	14.966	15.679	16.425	17.207
12 Endowed equity		12.857	13.469	14.111	14.783	15.487
13 PAT		1.437	1.505	1.577	1.652	1.731
14 Imputed equity credit		0.929	0.973	1.019	1.068	1.118
15 Endowed equity debit		(0836)	(0.876)	(0.917)	(0.961)	(1.007)
16 Adjusted PAT		1.530	1.602	1.679	1.759	1.842
17 Holding gain		0.612	0.641	0.672	0.704	0.737
18		2.142	2.244	2.351	2.463	2.580
19 ROIE		14.993%	14.993%	14.993%	14.993%	14.993%
Equity flows						
20 Imputed equity	−14.2857	(0.680)	(0.713)	(0.747)	(0.782)	17.207
21 Profit + HG		2.142	2.244	2.351	2.463	2.580
22 Equity flows	(14.286)	1.462	1.531	1.604	1.680	19.787
NPV at	14.993%	(0.0000)				
IRR		14.993%				

FINANCIAL DECISION-MAKING

local and UK tax rates of 40 per cent and 35 per cent respectively. The first eight rows show the situation in local currency. Note in particular that the imputed equity credit and the endowed equity debit have been calculated using a local pre-tax interest rate of 5 per cent. Profits are taxed at 40 per cent, but the imputed and endowed equity credits and debits are taxed at the UK rate. The local rate of return is shown in row 9.

Row 10 shows the FX rates. Their movement exactly reflects the difference in UK and local interest rates.

Rows 11 and 12 show the sterling value of imputed and endowed equity. Sterling profit after local tax is shown in the next row. The imputed and endowed equity adjustments are shown in rows 14 and 15, net of UK tax. Adjusted profits after tax are shown in row 16, while row 17 adds in the holding gain. The consequent sterling return on imputed equity of 15 per cent is shown in row 19.

The equity flows are shown in rows 20 to 22. Their IRR is also 15 per cent. Thus on the assumptions used a local return of 9.9 per cent will generate a sterling return of 15 per cent. The approach can be used to simulate any combination of differential interest rates and comparative levels of imputed and endowed equity. Once the relation has been established, the local return can be used in the pricing model, provided local interest rates are used for the imputed and endowed equity interest rate adjustments.

13.8 Relationship Profitability

Accurate cost estimates might be difficult to obtain when attempting to access the costs of generating customer deposits. A whole range of services are supplied to customers, and many banks' costing systems do not allow accurate costing by both product and customer. Moreover losses will be tolerated on some products to gain the profit on others. In such circumstances it may only be possible to look at a customer's profitability in total.

Problems such as these can be handled by the model, as shown in Table 13.8. Three types of assets are built into the model: fixed, personal loans and mortgage lending. The rest of the balance sheet is then derived using local capital and liquidity requirements.

Two additional sources of income are available from personal customers: firstly the income from the sale of insurance, mutual funds and similar services, which amount to £5, and, secondly, £400 of deposits gathered, on which interest of 8 per cent is paid, and shown as deposit

Pricing

TABLE 13.8 Customer Group Profitability

Local balance sheet			
Endowed equity	14.75	Cash (0.0%)	6.04
Secondary capital	0.00	Cash (7.75%)	38.64
	14.75	Government debt (6%)	26.56
Deposits	241.49	Mortgage lending	75.00
		Personal loans	100.00
		Fixed assets	10.00
Total liabilities	256.24	Total assets	256.24
Local profit and loss account			
Required ROIE	1.4715	Cash (0.0%)	0.0000
Deposits	28.9787	Cash (7.75%)	2.8979
Operating costs	8.0000	Government debt (6%)	1.5938
Deposit costs	32.0000	Deposit income	48.0000
Specific provision	0.0000	Fee income	5.0000
Int. end equity	0.0959	Imputed equity	0.0683
Second tier adj.	0.0146		57.5600
Local tax	0.8151	Revenue on asset	13.8158
Total costs	71.3758	Total revenue	71.3758

costs of £32. These are lent out to other divisions of the bank at 12 per cent and shown as deposit income of £48. Total divisional operating costs amount to £8.

With all these sources of income and associated costs, the model shows that personal lending and mortgage lending must generate £13.82. On combined lending of £175 this is a yield of only 7.9 per cent, which is 4.1 per cent below the local cost of funds. Since, in practice, the margins obtained from personal and mortgage lending are positive, this bank's personal banking activities are very profitable indeed.

13.9 Relative Risk

Every year banks have to write off a proportion of their loans or contingents, owing to the failure of some obligors. Experience usually gives a good guide to the proportions of the various categories of outstandings

FINANCIAL DECISION-MAKING

that have to be written off. Where it does not, judgement or even guesswork must be used.

A given category of lending can only be profitable if income is sufficient to cover write-offs as well as all other costs. Taking one year with another, such write-offs are inevitable, and for the purposes of the pricing model should be treated as specific tax-deductible costs. When this is done, all that happens is that the required margin or fee is increased by the write-off rate. Different categories of risk are accounted for by differing write-off levels.

From a tax point of view only write-offs of principal, payments made under guarantees or similar costs are tax-deductible. Interest or fees forgone are not tax-deductible, since profits automatically fall as a result of non-receipt. Such losses therefore cannot be incorporated into the cost structure. Nevertheless insolvency will cause loss of income, just as it will cause loss of principal.

It is just as likely that obligors will become insolvent at the beginning, middle or end of the year. On average therefore this is equivalent to mid-year insolvency. Generally this means that income from such entities will be earned for half the year. For example, it could be assessed that there is a 2 per cent probability of a particular group of obligors becoming insolvent during a year. Assuming no further income is received on insolvency, this means that only 99 per cent of legally due revenue are likely to be received from this group, and the break-even level of income must be grossed up by 100/0.99 to allow for this expected loss.

Table 13.9 shows the impact of failing to gross income up to reflect the

TABLE 13.9 Impact of Insolvency On Required Margins

Probability of insolvency (%)	Impact of principal	Total impact	Difference
0	13.50	13.50	–
1	14.50	14.57	0.07
2	15.50	15.66	0.16
3	16.50	16.75	0.25
4	17.50	17.86	0.36
5	18.50	18.97	0.47
6	19.50	20.10	0.60
7	20.50	21.24	0.90
8	21.50	22.40	0.90
9	22.50	25.56	1.06
10	23.50	24.74	1.24

Pricing

implications of insolvency. The no-risk yield of 13.5 per cent was generated, using a 10 per cent cost of funds. For every 1 per cent increase in the probability of insolvency, £1 is added to costs and hence to the required yield; this is shown under the Impact of principal. However, the total impact must reflect the probability of income not being received. When the probability of failure is 2 per cent, this is derived by dividing the yield of 15.5 per cent by 0.99 to obtain a fully adjusted yield of 15.66 per cent. At 0.16 per cent the difference between the two may appear minimal, but it is worth well over 1 per cent in terms of the return on equity, and should not be ignored.

In the discussion so far general provisions have been deliberately ignored. It was suggested in Chapter 7 (section 7.9) that under the BIS capital adequacy rules banks would be better off not making general provisions. Nevertheless, if they are still made, they are dealt with by incorporating them into the imputed equity ratio.

13.10 Bridging the Gap

'Bridging the Gap' sounds uncomplicated, and conceptually it is not particularly complex. A simple example has already been given in section 13.2, and indeed it illustrates the whole essence of the approach. If the earnings from a product or a business are inadequate, only a limited number of basic options are available. Prices or margins can be increased, costs rationalised, unit costs reduced by increased output, or efforts concentrated on the more profitable products. If none of these approaches work, then ultimately new business strategies will have to evolve, or the business be closed. Generation of the latter options is beyond the scope of this chapter, and their evaluation has already been considered.

Finding ways of closing the gaps in order to generate adequate returns calls for tactics rather than strategy. It is concerned with getting the best out of current activities rather than seeking new directions. Nevertheless product pricing is only one aspect of profit enhancement, particularly if current activities are in need of a major improvement. In such circumstances a more aggregated approach will often be necessary, at least as an initial step.

Gap analysis has two key objectives. The first is to assess combinations of income, costs, assets and contingents necessary to provide an adequate return on equity; and the second to compare the current situation with the target position, which may take several years to achieve, so

FINANCIAL DECISION-MAKING

TABLE 13.10 Gap Analysis: Balance Sheet Summary

	ACTUAL									TARGET							
	COMMERCIAL		TREASURY		PRIVATE		TOTAL		COMMERCIAL		TREASURY		PRIVATE		TOTAL		REAL %
	FFbn	Margin %	FFbn	Margin %	FFbn	Margin %	FFbn	Margin %	FFbn	Margin %	FFbn	Margin %	FFbn	Margin %	FFbn	Margin %	Increase

Cash
Government securities
Deposits with banks
Other reserve assets
Banking assets weighted : 0%
  : 10%
  : 20%
  : 50%
  : 100%

Total banking assets
Total risk-weighted banking assets
Fixed assets: Premises
  : Equipment
Total fixed assets
Contingents Weighted : %
  : %
  : %
  : %

Total contingents
Total risk-weighted contingents
TOTAL RISK-WEIGHTED ASSETS
Imputed equity
Endowed equity

GAP ANALYSIS KEY PERFORMANCE INDICATORS

ROI/S: Pre-tax
  : Post-tax
Return on RWA (pre-tax)
Net interest margin
Net Interest/risk-weighted banking assets
Fee income/risk-weighted contingent liabilities
NFBI/Total income
Costs/Income
Support services/Total costs
Real income per head
Real costs per head
Real profits (pre-tax) per head
Total staff

[168]

Pricing

TABLE 13.11 Gap Analysis: Profit Summary

	ACTUAL					TARGET			
	COMMERCIAL	TREASURY	PRIVATE	TOTAL		COMMERCIAL	TREASURY	PRIVATE	TOTAL	REAL % INCREASE
INTEREST INCOME										
Interest income (maybe split into several groups)										
Notional income from deposits										
Total interest income										
FUNDING COSTS										
Customer deposits										
Money market										
Notional charge from other departments										
Endowed equity debit										
Imputed equity credit										
Total funding costs										
NET INTEREST INCOME										
FEE INCOME										
Trade-related										
Merchant banking										
Traditional treasury										
New treasury										
Fund management/Trusts etc.										
Total fee income										
Total income before provisions										
PROVISIONS										
Total income after provisions										
OPERATING COSTS										
Excluding support services : Staff										
: Premises										
: Other										
Total non-support services costs										
Support Services : Staff										
: Premises										
: Other										
Total support services costs										
Total costs										
PBT										
Tax local										
Tax EE/IE										
PAT										

FINANCIAL DECISION-MAKING

facilitating judgement on the plausibility of the latter. An outline of how to achieve these objectives is given in Tables 13.10 and 13.11.

Balance sheet assets are shown in the first of these tables; liabilities have been suppressed to keep the table down to a manageable size. Required liquid assets are shown first, followed by banking assets analysed by risk weightings. Both sets of assets can be broken out in further categories if it is considered helpful and the data are available. Fixed assets and contingent liabilities are also shown, with the latter categorised by risk weightings. Finally imputed and endowed equity are noted.

All this information is shown for three businesses and the bank in total. Margins are also shown, or, strictly, fees in the case of contingents. Two situations are shown the current and the target positions.

Key performance indicators are given at the end of Table 13.10. They serve two interrelated functions. For example, the current cost:income ratio could be obviously too high, either in comparison to other of the bank's activities or in relation to competitors. Other information may indicate that costs rather than income are the problem. If so, an immediate line of attack is suggested. On the other hand, income per head may be too low, perhaps suggesting low margins or inadequate throughput.

Basically the profit and loss statement (Table 13.11) is derived from the balance sheet in the normal way. However, Notional income from deposits is credited to the business segment at money market rates, and then charged out to other departments at this rate under Notional charge from other departments. Otherwise the income aspects are straightforward. Operating costs are broken out into two broad categories – non-support service and support service costs. They are taken as approximations to variable and fixed costs respectively.

It is now a matter of examining how an acceptable return can be achieved in a realistic way. In assessing the improvements needed to achieve the target ROIE, interrelations between the variables must be allowed for. The impact on equity of increased assets is automatically incorporated. However, extra marketing and its support staff may be required, even if other costs remain fixed, as throughput is increased. Improved margins might only result from increased value added. This may involve improved systems, and additional or more highly paid staff. Significant increases in income will sometimes push margins down. These are just a few of the interrelationships that must be allowed for when exploring how adequate returns can be achieved.

14

THE COST OF EQUITY REVISITED

14.1 Introduction

At the end of Chapter 5 the concept of a weighted cost of capital (WCC) was introduced. On the basis of the CAPM it was shown that the WCC was invariant to the mix of equity and debt. Consequently the lower the equity to debt ratio the higher the COE, and vice versa. In the subsequent chapters this consequence of the theory was ignored, as there was already enough complication, but now it must be dealt with.

14.2 Bank Betas

Before the COE specific to a particular situation can be considered, a starting point must be established. A bank's COE is derived from its Beta, which in turn is partly dependent upon the bank's capital structure. Estimates of UK bank Betas are readily available, and Table 14.1 lists those for a number of UK and other banks.

TABLE 14.1 Selected Bank Betas

	_____ Year end _____						
	1982	1983	1984	1985	1986	*30.6.87*	*31.10.88*
Lloyds	0.78	0.85	0.88	1.00	1.31	1.27	1.14
Barclays	0.89	0.94	0.92	1.03	1.15	1.10	0.88
Nat West	0.85	0.90	0.87	0.90	1.08	1.12	0.98
Midland	–	–	–	–	–	0.85	0.98
Citicorp	1.15	1.10	1.10	1.25	1.25	–	–
Morgan	0.90	0.85	0.90	1.05	1.10	–	–
Security Pacific	0.95	1.00	1.00	0.99	1.15	–	–
Bankers Trust	0.90	0.95	1.05	1.10	1.20	–	–
Average	0.92	0.94	0.96	1.05	1.18	–	–

FINANCIAL DECISION-MAKING

The first aspect to note is the lack of stability in the Betas. For the period 1982 to 1986 they showed a marked upward trend. Subsequently the UK banks' Betas declined, but were generally higher than their 1982 values. Clearly current Betas cannot automatically be taken as a guide to the future. An attempt must be made to explain the movements, perhaps in terms of changes in equity to debt ratios, the ratio of LDC debt to equity, or perhaps a general change in the structure of the banks' assets and business activities. In practice it is highly unlikely that an accurate quantification of the changes will be possible. Judgement must come into play, and a view taken of the riskiness of the project being undertaken compared to that of banks whose Betas have exhibited less instability.

14.3 Calculating the Cost of Equity

Once a view has been taken on Beta, it can then be related to an appropriate capital structure. In all likelihood this will be the one pertaining over the period used to calculate Beta. On the basis of the CAPM the WCC should remain constant. Thus, as the equity to debt ratio changes, the new COE can be calculated.

Tax relief on interest payments, however, tends to favour a low equity to debt ratio, for a higher ratio will increase the ROE. If tax is ignored and the Beta of debt remains constant, the COE will increase exactly in line with the ROE, and nothing is gained by increasing debt. Several examples are introduced to show what happens when taxation is introduced. Various possibilities are depicted in Table 14.2. First comes a balance sheet, which is assumed to be consistent with an observed COE and equity Beta of 14 per cent and 1.0 respectively. Additionally it is assumed that both debt and deposits have a Beta of ⅓. By the conventional calculation, the assets' Beta is $0.06 \times 1.0 + 0.94 \times (1/3)$, which is 0.3733.

Next three sets of profit and loss accounts are shown. These are associated with equity ratios of 6 per cent, 7 per cent and 5 per cent. The first of each set shows expected profits and ROEs. The second of each set shows what happens when the return on total assets increases 1 per cent. Take the equity at 6 per cent column as an example. The assets have a Beta of 0.3733 while debt and deposits have a Beta of 0.3333. Consequently, if the return on assets increases 1 per cent, i.e. from £10.8m to £11.8m, the interest on borrowing increases by 0.3333/0.3733. Interest rates therefore increase from 10 per cent to 10.893 per cent, and the cost of borrowing increases from £9.4m to £10.239m. Profits before tax

The Cost of Equity Revisited

TABLE 14.2 Corporate Tax and the Cost of Equity

Balance sheet				Profit and loss accounts				
			Equity 6%		Equity 7%		Equity 5%	
Assets	100	Income	10.800	11.800	10.800	11.800	10.800	11.800
Equity	6	Costs	(9.400)	(10.239)	(9.300)	(10.130)	9.500	(10.348)
Second tier	4	PBT	1.400	1.561	1.500	1.670	1.300	1.452
Capital	10	Tax	(0.560)	(0.624)	0.600	(0.668)	(0.520)	(0.581)
Deposits	90	PAT	0.840	0.936	0.900	1.002	0.780	0.871
	100							
		ROIE	14.000	15.607	12.857	14.311	15.600	17.421
		Beta	1.000		0.905		1.133	
		COE %	14.000		13.429		14.800	

Note: Beta is calculated from Beta (E) = Beta (A) + [Beta (A) − Beta (D)] $\frac{D}{E}$.

See Chapter 5 for derivation.

increase from £1.4m to £1.561m, and after tax from £0.840m to £0.936m. Hence the ROE increases from 14 per cent to 15.6 per cent. The other two sets of profit and loss accounts are similarly calculated.

As the equity to borrowings ratio changes, so does the equity Beta. This is shown in the table and is calculated in the normal way (see Chapter 5). Moreover the Beta calculations are consistent with the noted ROE variabilities. In the first case the ROE increases 1.607 per cent, while in the next two it increases 1.454 per cent and 1.821 per cent respectively. Dividing these latter ROE variations by the first gives ratios that equal the corresponding Betas, so that, in this respect the results conform to the theory. The Betas are then used to calculate the COE in the second two cases.

The consequences are clear: when equity increases the COE does not fall as much as the ROE, and vice versa. Thus, provided interest rates remain invariant to the equity borrowing ratio, the lower the equity ratio the higher the surplus return to shareholders. This latter assumption is almost certainly a reasonable approximation for most banks, given their limited scope for varying the equity ratio. Consequently banks with lower equity ratios will tend to earn their shareholders a better return.

Given the constancy of the WCC, the COE can also be calculated from this relation. In the first case the WCC is:

$$0.06 \times 14\% + 0.94 \times 10\% = 10.24\%$$

[173]

FINANCIAL DECISION-MAKING

In the second case the COE can be calculated from:

0.07 × COE + 0.93 × 10% = 10.24%

to obtain a COE of 13.429 per cent.

When the WCC itself is used for discounting, interest payments are excluded from the profits. In the initial case the appropriate cashflow would be £10.8m. After tax at 40 per cent this becomes £6.48m, to give a return on total assets, or capital, of 6.48 per cent. When calculating the WCC for discounting, use the net of tax interest rate. This gives a WCC of:

0.06 × 14% + 0.94 × 6%

which is 6.48 per cent.

14.4 Implications for Project Appraisal

Most of the situations considered in previous chapters have a more or less constant capital structure. So, once the COE has been determined, the equity flows can be discounted at the same rate each year. Not all situations, however, will be this straightforward. For example, when goodwill is paid on an acquisition, the initial equity ratio will, from the shareholders' viewpoint, be significantly higher than the subsequent incremental equity ratios. Consequently the initial COE will be relatively low, and then the average COE will continually increase.

Taking this case as an example, calculate the average COE every year. This is not as complex as it seems, for the initial COE is known, while the incremental cost of equity is constant. Therefore calculating a weighted average is straightforward and will take little time using a PC. However, beware when calculating the initial COE.

Without goodwill, assets might be £100m, supported by £6m of equity. If goodwill of £4m is paid, then assets become £104m, including the goodwill, while equity becomes £10m, though only £6m of equity will be recognised for capital adequacy purposes. With assets of £100m a £1m increase in profits (pre-tax and interest) increases the ROAs by 1 per cent. With goodwill of £4m the ROAs only increases by 1/1.04 per cent. Hence, when the £4m of goodwill is included, Beta must fall by 1/1.04; the same applies to the WCC.

In the acquisition example the average ratio of shareholders' equity

The Cost of Equity Revisited

plus second tier capital to assets varies each year. Generally this is not the case; often the equity plus second tier ratio will remain more or less constant. Usually it will be fixed somewhere in the range of 8 per cent to 11 per cent of RWAs.

Within that ratio, however, the equity proportion might vary. If it does, an estimate, in principle, of the COE can be made each year. The Beta of the assets will remain more or less constant over the evaluation period, so that the relation between the equity Beta and the asset's Beta can be used to estimate the former. Alternatively the WCC remains constant and the relation between this, the COE and interest can be used to estimate the COE.

Table 14.3 shows how discounting is done when the COE is changing. Four projects are considered. The first requires an equity outlay of £100m, has a 10 per cent COE and generates a 10 per cent IRR. All the others have a 15 per cent COE and generate IRRs of 15 per cent. Their investment outlays are £10m, £11m and £12m respectively. Total and incremental equities are shown in rows 1 and 2. The average COE is shown in row 3. In year 4, for example, it is calculated so:

$$10\% \times [100/133] + 15\% [33/133]$$

to give 11.24 per cent. In year 3 the discount rate is $1.10 \times 1.1045 \times 1.1087$, which is 1.3470.

Project and total cashflows are shown in rows 5 to 9. The penultimate row shows the cashflow discounted at the average COE. On this basis their NPV is zero, as required.

TABLE 14.3   Varying Cost of Equity (£m)

Year end	0	1	2	3	4	5
1 Total equity	100.00	110.00	121.00	133.00	133.00	0.00
2 Incremental equity	100.00	10.00	11.00	12.00	0.00	
3 Average COE	10.00%	10.45%	10.87%	11.24%	11.24%	
4 Discount rate		1.1000	1.2150	1.3470	1.4985	1.6669
5 Project (ROE = 10%)	(100.00)	10.00	10.00	10.00	10.00	110.00
6 Project (ROE = 15%)		(10.00)	1.50	1.50	1.50	11.50
7 Project (ROE = 15%)			(11.00)	1.65	1.65	12.65
8 Project (ROE = 15%)				(12.00)	1.80	13.80
9 Cashflow	(100.00)	0.00	0.50	1.15	14.95	147.95
DCF at av. COE	(100.0000)	0.0000	0.4115	0.8537	9.9769	88.7578
NPV at av. COE	0.0000					

FINANCIAL DECISION-MAKING

14.5 An Example: Property Evaluation

An example using variable COE's is given in Table 14.4. The key assumptions are:

- Initial property value £100m.
- Equity ratio 40 per cent.
- Property appreciation 10 per cent p.a.
- Cost of capital 15 per cent.
- Cost of debt 7.5 per cent.
- Rent saved 5 per cent of property's value.

The first part of the table depicts the balance sheets reflecting the above assumptions. In year 3, for example, the value of the property has increased from £100m to £121m. On the liabilities side of the balance sheet it is represented by £48.4m of equity contributed in cash by the shareholders, £21m of revaluation reserves and £51.6m of deposits.

Next comes the cashflow statement on the assumption that the property is 100 per cent equity-financed. This shows an initial outlay of £100m, followed by the rent saved in the next three years. In the final year the property is sold for £133.1m. When discounted at 15 per cent, these cashflows generate a zero net present value.

Now consider the equity flows when 40 per cent of the property's value is equity-funded. The constituents are shown in the final section of the table (rows 18–24). First comes rent saved. Next comes the equity put up by the shareholders. Their initial investment is £40m, but each year they must increase their contributions in line with the property's increased value.

At the end of the final year the property is sold for £133.1m. Of this, £46.76m is used to repay debt, leaving £86.34m for the shareholders (£53.24m in equity contributions plus a capital gain of £33.1m).

Finally interest payments are shown. The sum of these items gives the annual receipts from or payments to shareholders. However, before the project's worth to the shareholders can be evaluated, the appropriate COE must be calculated.

The opening equity to debt ratio is 40:60, so that the COE is 26.25 per cent (row 14). Next the COE calculation for the final year is shown. The opening balance sheet shows imputed equity of £48.4m and revaluation reserves of £21m, so that total equity amounts to £69.4m. Total opening debt is £51.6m. Therefore the opening debt to equity ratio is 42.64:57.36 and the COE is derived from:

The Cost of Equity Revisited

TABLE 14.4 Property Evaluations using Weighted Cost of Capital (GBP,M)

		Year 1	2	3	4
	Opening balance sheets				
1	Property	100.0000	110.0000	121.0000	133.1000
2	Imputed equity	40.0000	44.0000	48.4000	53.2400
3	Revaluation reserve	0.0000	10.0000	21.0000	33.1000
4	Deposits	60.0000	56.0000	51.6000	46.7600
5	Total liabilities	100.0000	110.0000	121.0000	133.1000
6	Rent saved		5.0000	5.5000	6.0500
7	Equity	(100.0000)			133.1000
8	Cashflow	(100.0000)	5.0000	5.5000	139.1500
9	Net present value at 0.1500		0.0000		
10	Internal rate of return		0.1500		
	Cost of equity				
11	Total equity %		0.4000	0.4909	0.5736
12	Debt %		0.6000	0.5091	0.4264
13	Weighted cost of capital		0.1500	0.1500	0.1500
14	Cost of equity		0.2625	0.2278	0.2058
15	Interest rate		0.0750	0.0750	0.0750
16	Annual discount rate		1.2625	1.2278	1.2058
17	Cumulative discount rate		1.2625	1.5501	1.8690
	Equity flows				
18	Rent		5.0000	5.5000	6.0500
19	Incremental IE	(40.0000)	(4.0000)	(4.4000)	(4.8400)
20	Release of IE				53.2400
21	Capital gain				33.1000
22	Interest		(4.5000)	(4.2000)	(3.8700)
23	Equity flows	(40.0000)	(3.5000)	(3.1000)	83.6800
24	Discounted equity flows	(40.0000)	(2.7723)	(1.9999)	44.7722

Net present value   0.0000
Growth   Rent   IE%   Interest
1.1000   0.0500   0.4000   0.0750

FINANCIAL DECISION-MAKING

$$15\% = 0.5736 \times \text{COE} + 0.4264 \times 7.5\%$$

that is:

$$\text{COE} = 20.58\%$$

Each year therefore an appropriate COE has been calculated. Thus the first year's equity flow of £(3.5)m is discounted by 1.2625, while in year 3, for example, the equity flow of £83.68m is discounted by 1.2625 × 1.2278 × 1.2058, which equals 1.8690 (row 17). The discounted equity flows are shown in row 24. When summed, their net present value is zero, as expected.

14.6 Summary

No easy or straightforward answers have been given in this chapter, owing to the nature of the problem. What does seem clear is that fairly large changes in the equity ratio do not have a great impact on the COE. Thus a 40 per cent increase in the equity ratio from 5 per cent to 7 per cent only increased the COE from 13.4 per cent to 14.8 per cent. Taking account of COE changes of 1 percentage point or less is clearly spurious. Once they exceed 2 percentage points, then it is probably worth undertaking a sensitivity analysis. Even then it would probably be more fruitful to devote the effort to improving or validating the cost and income projections. Only in circumstances when large deviations from the typical COE are anticipated will it be worth attempting to estimate project or asset specific Betas. Even tl.en they will often have to be little more than guesses.

INDEX

Bank of England, 61, 62, 95, 103
Bank of England/USA Federal Reserve: 'Convergence of Capital Adequacy in the UK and US', 55
Bank of Spain, 133, 148, 159
bank regulation, 55
   risk-weighted assets, 55–6
      calculation of, 57–9
      conventional contingents, 56
      credit conversion factors, 56, 65–6
      estimating credit exposure, 56–7
      interest rate and FX contingents, 56–7
banks' capital adequacy
   deductions from capital, 61
   first tier capital, 59
   minimum capital ratio, 61
   relations summarising, 61
   second tier capital, 59
      general provisions, 60
      hybrid debt instruments, 60
      revaluation reserves, 59–60
      subordinated debt, 60
      undisclosed reserves, 59
Barclays de Zoete Wedd: Equity-Gilt study, 28, 33, 35
basic banking model
   back to accounting profits, 68–9, 70
   basic equity flow model, 69–70
   case study: an acquisition, 88–91
   cashflow revisited, 70
   closure, 91–2
   dealing with existing debt, 108–11
      bond valuation, 111–12
   equity injections, 75–6
   example, 81–4
   free funding, 80–1

goodwill, 86–7, 92
international dimensions, *see* international dimensions of basic banking model
minorities, 87–8
non-consolidated investments, 88
opportunity costs, 72–5
   of subsidiary, 73–4
question of equity flows or cashflows, 67–8
sale, 92–3
second tier capital, 76–7
   general provisions, 79–80
   opportunity costs, 77–8
   treatment, 78–80
terminal values, 84
   dividends in perpetuity, 84
   recommended approach, 85
   sale of business, 84–5
Beta, 31–7 *passim*, 49, 50, 51, 173, 174, 175
   bank Betas, 171–2
   estimation of, 34
Brazilian debt, 115–19 *passim*

capital asset pricing model (CAPM), 48–51, 171, 172
   critique, 35–7
   practical applications, 33–4
      risk premium, 33
   theoretical framework, 30–3
   risk, 32, 56
capital, *see* banks' capital adequacy
cashflow analysis, traditional, 67
   bygones are bygones, 45–6
   cashflow and shareholder value, 40–1
   distinction between profits and cashflows, 45

profits, balance sheets and cashflows, 41–5
reasons for, 38–40
see also weighted cost of capital
Committee on Banking Regulations and Supervisory Practices (BIS) report, 55
capital requirements, 59
risk weights, 59, 80, 86, 88, 167
rules and regulations, 59, 80, 86, 88, 167
cost of equity (COE), 37, 48–9, 52, 160, 171, 178
bank Betas, 171–2
calculating, 172–4
example of property evaluation, 176–8
implications for project appraisal, 174–5
measuring returns on, 25–6
arithmetic average, 26–7
geometric mean or income reinvested method, 27–8
UK – an alternative approach, 28–30

Davies, Gavyn, 33
debt-forgiveness, 108, 119–20
debt swaps
alternative approach, 116–17
taxation, 119
valuing debt, 117–18
valuing property, 118–19
comparative economics, 112–14
debt bond swaps, 105
additional provisions, 108
expected values, 108
new monies, 107, 113, 114, 118
provisions are bygones, 105–7
see also, basic banking model, dealing with existing debt
debt equity swaps, 114–16
development banks, 63
discounted cashflow analysis
accounting data, 5–6
depreciation methods, 5–6
economic depreciation, 12–14
measuring profitability, 5, 6
net present value (NPV), 10–11, 12
of irregular cashflow, 12
present value, 7–9, 11
time dimension, 6–7
true rate of return, 12

equity
fundamental constituent of capital, 59
see also, cost of equity

Financial Times, 36
fixed asset expenditure evaluation, 130
investment in property, 134–5
example, 139–43
problem of insufficient secondary capital, 137–8
property revaluations, 135–7
sale of premises, 138–9
plant and equipment, 130–1
supporting balance sheet, 131–3
revaluations as contributions to first tier capital, 144–5

goodwill, 61, 86–7, 92, 174
'Group of Ten' countries, 55
central banks, 56

Housing Corporation, 63

Ibbotson and Sinquefield, 26
integrated model
balance sheet and contingents, 124, 125
basic structure, 121–2
environmental assumptions, 122–4
equity, 129
net interest income, 124, 126–7
profit and loss account, 127–8
internal rate of return (IRR), 12, 175
international dimensions of basic banking model
additional considerations, 94
example of FX and holding gains, 95–8
FX movements, 95
holding gains, 95
inflation, 98
interest rates, 94, 98–9
local v domestic accounting, 100
project appraisal, 99
example, 100–2

London Bullion Market Association, 63
London Business School, 33

Merrett and Sykes, 28
Mexican Bond for Mexican Debt Swap, 105, 107, 111, 113
Midland Bank, 144

Index

National Westminster Bank, 144

Organisation for Economic Co-operation and Development (OECD), 62
   banks, 56, 58, 59, 62
   public sector entities (PSEs), 63

price/earnings (PE) ratio
   question of meaningfulness, 22–4
   UK, 1988, 24, 32
pricing
   average and marginal cost pricing
      cost of funds, 162
      external pricing, 159–60
      internal marginal cost pricing, 160–1
   bridging the gap, 167–70
   derivation of basic model, 149–54
   extension of model, 154–7
   fee income, 157–9
   local and domestic returns, 162–4
   rationale, 146
   relationship profitability, 164–5
   relative risk, 165–7
   supporting balance sheet revisited, 146–9
      pricing a loan, 149

shareholder value
   earnings and dividends compared, 16–18
   average and marginal earnings compared, 19–20
   cashflow and, 40–1
   price/earnings ratio, *see* separate entry
   rationale, 15–16
   real and nominal returns, 21–2
   retained profits v dividends, 18–19
Standard and Poor's Composition Index, 26

United Kingdom
   building societies, 63
   public sector entities (PSEs), 63
USA Federal Reserve, *see* Bank of England/USA Federal Reserve
US Treasury, 105

Wadhwani, Sushill, 33
weighed cost of capital, 47–8, 171–5 *passim*
   CAPM and, 48–51
   equity flows, 46–7
   property evaluations using, 177
   repayment assumptions, 51–2